BEHAVIOURAL ASPECTS OF AUDITORS' EVIDENCE EVALUATION

To Mohamed

Behavioural Aspects of Auditors' Evidence Evaluation

A Belief Revision Perspective

MAGDA ABOU-SEADA
Middlesex University
MAGDY ABDEL-KADER
University of Essex

ASHGATE

© Magda Abou-Seada and Magdy Abdel-Kader 2003

All rights reserved. No part of this publication may be reproduced, stored in a retrieval system, or transmitted in any form or by any means, electronic, mechanical, photocopying, recording or otherwise without the prior permission of the publisher.

The authors have asserted their moral right under the Copyright, Designs and Patents Act, 1988, to be identified as the authors of this work.

Published by
Ashgate Publishing Limited
Gower House
Croft Road
Aldershot
Hants
GU11 3HR
England

Ashgate Publishing Ltd
Suite 420
101 Cherry Street
Burlington, VT 05401-4405
USA

Ashgate website: http://www.ashgate.com

British Library Cataloguing in Publication Data
Abou-Seada, Magda
 Behavioural aspects of auditors' evidence evaluation : a
 belief revision perspective
 1. Auditing - Methodology
 I. Title II. Abdel-Kader, Magdy G.
 657 .4'5

ISBN 0 7546 3221 0

Library of Congress Cataloging-in-Publication Data
Abou-Seada, Magda.
 Behavioural aspects of auditors' evidence evaluation: a belief revision perspective /
 Magda Abou-Seada and Magdy Abdel-Kader.
     p. cm
 Includes bibliographical references and index.
 ISBN 0-7546-3221-0 (alk. paper)
  1. Auditing, Analytical review. 2. Auditors' reports. 3. Auditing--Decision making. 4. Behaviourism (Psychology) I. Abdel-Kader, Magdy G. II. Title

HF5567 .A25 2003
657'.452--dc21

2002034500

Printed and bound in Great Britain by Antony Rowe Ltd, Chippenham, Wiltshire

Contents

List of Tables		*viii*
List of Figures		*ix*
Preface		*x*

1   Introduction and Overview   1

Context for the Study	1
The Audit Process and Evidence Evaluation	1
The Belief Revision Process	5
Evidence Evaluation Approaches in the UK Auditing Standards	7
Aims of the Study	9
Research Questions	10
Structure of the Book	10

2   The Belief-Adjustment as a Model of the Belief Revision Approach   13

Introduction	13
The Contrast/Surprise Model and its Predictions	13
The Belief-Adjustment Model and its Predictions	15
Advantages of the Belief-Adjustment Model	19
The Validity of the Predictions of the Contrast/Surprise and Belief-Adjustment Models	22
Conclusions	31

3   Factors Affecting Auditors' Belief Revisions   33

Introduction	33
Belief Formation	33
Confirmation Bias	38
Diagnostic Content of Evidence	39
Expertise	41
Professional Scepticism	44
Motivational Factors	45
Cognitive Factors	46
Conclusions	47

4	**Empirical Research Design**	49
	Introduction	49
	Aim of Empirical Study and Research Questions	49
	Research Methodology	50
	Conclusions	60
5	**Results of Interviews: Auditors' Approaches in Evaluating Evidence**	63
	Introduction	63
	The Evidence Evaluation Approach Followed by Auditors	63
	The Evidence Evaluation Approach in Case of New vs. Continuing Clients	69
	The Evidence Evaluation Approach in Case of Small vs. Large Clients	71
	Conclusions	72
6	**Results of Interviews: Factors Affecting Auditors' Evaluation of Evidence**	73
	Introduction	73
	Formation of the Initial Belief	73
	Expertise	84
	Confirmation Bias	85
	Professional Scepticism and Conservatism	89
	Diagnostic Content of Evidence	90
	Evidence Order	91
	Evaluation Mode	93
	Time and Cost	95
	Conclusions	96
7	**Results of Experiment**	99
	Introduction	99
	Basis of Comparisons	99
	Demographic Information About Participants	100
	Method of Analysis	101
	Differences Between the Open Mind and Belief Revision Approaches	102
	Differences Between Evidence Evaluation Modes	109
	Comparing Risk Assessment and the Initial Belief	115
	Conclusions	117

8	**Discussion and Conclusions**	**121**
	Introduction	121
	Findings of the Empirical Study	121
	Implications of the Findings of the Empirical Study	134
	Areas for Future Research	138
Bibliography		*141*
Appendices		*151*
Index		*165*

List of Tables

2.1	Order effect predictions of the belief-adjustment model	18
2.2	Summary of auditing studies on the contrast/surprise model	24
2.3	Summary of auditing studies on the belief-adjustment model	26
4.1	Personal information of interviewees	53
7.1	The experimental groups	100
7.2	Years of experience of participants in the experiment	101
7.3	Mean experiment time, additional time, and final opinion	104
7.4	Mann-Whitney U test in comparing the belief revision and open mind approaches	105
7.5	Chi-square test in comparing the belief revision and open mind approaches	106
7.6	Mann-Whitney U test in comparing the evidence evaluation modes	110
7.7	Chi-square test in comparing the evidence evaluation modes	111
7.8	Mean beliefs of participants in the B-SbS and B-EoS groups	113
7.9	Chi-square test in comparing the initial belief and risk assessment	115
8.1	Summary of main findings of the experiment	128

List of Figures

1.1	Evidence in the audit process	3
1.2	Stages of the audit process	4
1.3	Relationship between audit procedures, evidence and the auditor's opinion	8
2.1	The audit planning task	21
5.1	The belief revision approach in evidence evaluation	67
5.2	The open mind approach in evidence evaluation	68

Preface

This book is based on the PhD studies of the first author carried out at the University of the West of England, Bristol. The interest in the field of auditors' evidence evaluation has been stimulated by previous research on information processing. Belief revision has been the focus of auditing research since the introduction of a model for belief revision called the contrast/surprise model, lately revised to be the belief-adjustment model. This model has been described as a theory of belief revision.

The main aim of this study was to investigate the auditing practice to find out whether the belief revision approach is employed in evidence evaluation, and whether there are any benefits from employing this approach. To achieve this aim two research methodologies were employed; a survey research and an experimental study. The survey research involved carrying out personal interviews with 12 experienced auditors to explore the process of evidence evaluation in practice.

The findings of the interviews led to the design of the experimental study that involved conducting a laboratory experiment to investigate a number of issues related to the belief revision approach. Participants in the experiment were 64 practising auditors.

Although the authors have both made contributions to the work, the contribution of the first author is paramount. The contribution of the second author is limited to the conversion of the work to its current format.

This research benefited from the help and support of many people. We would greatly like to thank Professor Roger Hussey (University of Windsor) and Dr Ursula Lucas (University of the West of England, Bristol) for their advice, guidance, support and encouragement during the course of the study and afterwards. The helpful comments of Professor David Hatherly (University of Edinburgh) and Dr David Bence (University of the West of England, Bristol) must also be acknowledged. We would also like to thank members of the academic staff at the University of the West of England, Bristol who took part in the pilot testing of the empirical study and those who provided advice on statistical matters. Thanks are also due to participants at several of the British Accounting Association and European Accounting Association conferences for their helpful comments and advice. The help of Dr Khaled Abdala (University of Essex) in the preparation of this book is also appreciated. Finally, we gratefully acknowledge the financial support granted by the Egyptian Government to complete this research.

Dr Magda Abou-Seada
Dr Magdy Abdel-Kader
July, 2002

Chapter 1

Introduction and Overview

Context for the Study

The main purpose of this study is to investigate whether auditors follow a belief revision approach in their evaluation of evidence, and whether there are any benefits from following such an approach particularly with respect to the efficiency and effectiveness of the audit process.

The following points are addressed in this chapter:
- The audit process and evidence evaluation.
- The belief revision process.
- Evidence evaluation in the UK auditing standards.
- Aims of the study.
- Research questions.
- Structure of the book.

The Audit Process and Evidence Evaluation

Auditing is described as a sequential process of evidence gathering and evaluation with the aim of giving an independent opinion about the financial statements (Gibbins, 1984; Felix and Kinney, 1982; and Cushing and Loebbecke, 1986). Auditors base their opinion about a client's financial statements on the evidence collected during the course of the audit. The process of collecting evidence should follow a defined methodology to ensure that the evidence collected is relevant, reliable and sufficient. Any efficient and effective method that can be used in the search for and evaluation of such evidence would greatly aid auditors' decision-making.

One of the main aims of most accounting research in general is to improve decisions made by both accountants and users of accounting information (Waller and Jiambalva, 1984). This can be achieved by a better understanding of human information processing in accounting. The aim to understand and improve auditors' decision-making has been generally accepted as the goal of audit judgement research that includes evidence search and evaluation (Libby, 1981). Evidence search and evaluation are the centre of the audit process, and the efficiency and effectiveness of an audit depend to a great extent on evidence planning judgements concerning the nature, extent, and timing of procedures (Mock and Wright, 1993).

The manner in which evidence is evaluated and integrated with prior beliefs and other evidence can have a very practical effect on audit judgements and subsequent actions (Hooper and Trotman, 1996). Regardless of the differences between the local regulatory environments of different countries, it is not possible to complete an audit without obtaining relevant and reliable evidence (Power, 1992).

Despite the importance of audit judgement research, this type of research is still 'unable to develop the symbolic and justificational dimension of the audit process within the constraints of its theoretical framework'(Power, 1995, p. 317). In addition, auditing research in the UK has been slow to develop in recent years compared to the US (Gwilliam, 1987).

A few studies have attempted to study the audit decision-making process in the UK and, whilst, those studies provide valuable insights into aspects of auditing, they do not allow an overview of the entire audit process (Turley and Cooper, 1991). For example, Kirkham (1992) looked at the effect of environmental cues on the audit process, Power (1992) focused on evidence sampling, Hatherly et al. (1998) and Innes et al. (1997) were concerned with the audit report, and Humphrey and Moizer (1990) looked at the nature of auditing in terms of the diversity of roles that audit activities can serve.

Humphrey and Moizer (1990) indicated that accounting research in general has highlighted the social nature of accounting and the diversity of roles and functions that accounting performs. However, they indicted that 'there has been little attempt to apply this literature to a consideration of the nature of audit work and the processes of audit judgement'(Humphrey and Moizer, 1990, p. 217).

Some UK studies provided descriptions of the process of evidence search and evaluation. A useful description of evidence search and evaluation in the audit process is that provided by Spicer and Oppenheim et al. (1990). Figure 1.1 illustrates that various types of evidence are gathered from different sources according to the desired quantities and audit objectives. All these factors relate to the audit process which undergoes three main steps; planning, collection of evidence, and formation of an opinion. The planning will include understanding of the business, assessing risk and materiality, understanding and evaluating internal control, determining the appropriate audit approach and procedures, and segmenting the audit process or dividing the financial statement into segments to determine the appropriate evidence for each segment. Collection of evidence is mainly from tests of controls and substantive testing. Formation of an opinion involves aggregating evidence, an overall review of the financial statements, and finally coming to an opinion.

```
┌─────────────┐
│  Sources of │
│   evidence  │
└──────┬──────┘
       │            ┌─────────────┐
       │            │   Desired   │
       │            │quantities(and)│      ┌─────────────┐
       │            │ problems) of│      │    Audit    │
       │            │   evidence  │      │  objectives │
       │            └──────┬──────┘      └──────┬──────┘
       ▼                   │                     │
┌─────────────┐            │                     │
│   Types of  │            │                     │
│   evidence  │            │                     │
└──────┬──────┘            │                     │
       │                   │                     │
┌──────┼───────────────────┼─────────────────────┼──────┐
│      ▼                   ▼                     ▼      │
│             THE AUDIT PROCESS                         │
│                                                       │
│ ┌──────────┐     ┌──────────────────┐    ┌──────────┐│
│ │ Planning │────▶│   Collection of  │───▶│Forming an││
│ │decisions │     │     evidence     │    │  opinion ││
│ └──────────┘     └──────────────────┘    └──────────┘│
└───────────────────────────────────────────────────────┘
```

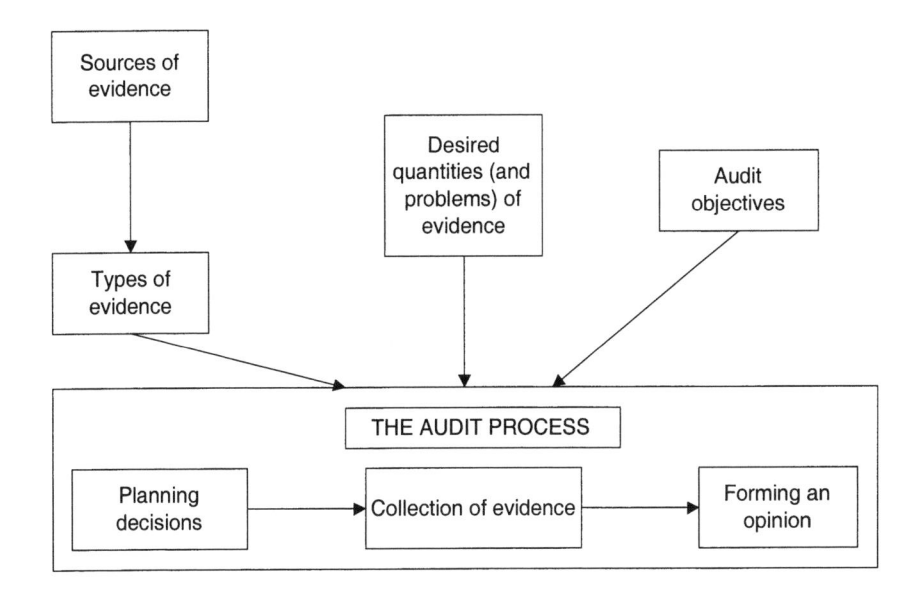

Figure 1.1 Evidence in the audit process
Source: Spicer and Oppenheim, 1990, p. 50.

Another description that expands on auditors' evidence search and evaluation is that suggested by Sherer and Kent (1983) and illustrated in figure 1.2. According to this description, auditors first conduct a priori appraisal of the internal control system based on a review of the company's procedures and discussions with client's personnel. Auditors then carry out compliance tests to make sure that the system works as expected from the priori appraisal. If the system was found to be reliable, auditors move on to do substantive tests. If serious failures were found in the internal control systems, auditors make recommendations to the management to implement new procedures which, in turn, are subjected to tests. After carrying out the substantive tests, if the accounts were found to be true and fair, an unqualified audit report is issued. However, if the accounts were found to include material error, auditors would ask the management to make appropriate adjustments after which an unqualified report is issued. If the management did not make the appropriate adjustments a qualified report is issued.

Although the previous descriptions provide some insight into the audit process in general, they do not help in developing a detailed framework of the process of evidence search and evaluation. Auditors collect evidence from many and varying sources and of different weight and reliability. The way that auditors integrate various pieces of evidence is not reflected in the structured descriptions of figures 1.1 or 1.2.

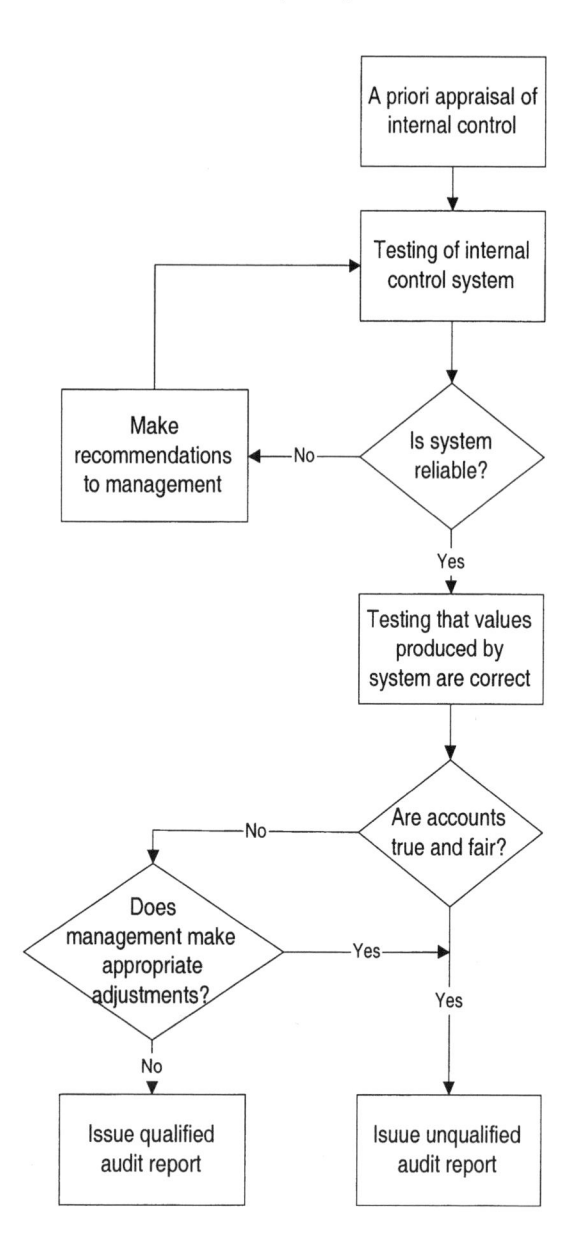

```
                    ┌─────────────────────┐
                    │ A priori appraisal of│
                    │  internal control   │
                    └──────────┬──────────┘
                               │
                               ▼
       ┌──────────────────► ┌─────────────────────┐
       │                    │ Testing of internal │
       │                    │   control system    │
       │                    └──────────┬──────────┘
       │                               │
       │                               ▼
┌──────┴──────────┐            ◇ Is system ◇
│      Make       │◄────No──── ◇ reliable? ◇
│ recommendations │            ◇           ◇
│  to management  │                  │
└─────────────────┘                  Yes
                                     │
                                     ▼
                        ┌─────────────────────┐
                        │  Testing that values│
                        │     produced by     │
                        │  system are correct │
                        └──────────┬──────────┘
                                   │
                                   ▼
                          ◇ Are accounts ◇
              ┌───No──── ◇ true and fair? ◇
              │                 │
              ▼                 Yes
      ◇ Does          ◇         │
      ◇ management    ◇──Yes──► │
      ◇ make appropriate◇       │
      ◇ adjustments?  ◇         │
              │                 │
             No                Yes
              ▼                 ▼
      ┌──────────────┐   ┌──────────────┐
      │Issue qualified│   │Isuue unqualified│
      │ audit report  │   │  audit report  │
      └──────────────┘   └──────────────┘
```

Figure 1.2 Stages of the audit process
Source: Sherer and Kent, 1983, p. 53.

Recent pressures on auditors to perform the audit more efficiently highlight the importance of being aware of different evidence evaluation approaches. The results of the interviews reported in Humphrey and Moizer's (1990) study indicated that auditing time nowadays is at a minimum and this time has to be used as effectively as possible to perform more efficient audits. It has been stated by one of the interviewees in Humphrey and Moizer's (1990, p. 230) study that:

> The pressure on time caused by fees has forced people into sitting down at the outset and thinking about what extra things they can cut out without affecting the audit quality.

Focusing on evidence search approaches might be very useful in helping auditors to perform the audit more efficiently without affecting its quality. The development of a general approach to the process of acquiring audit evidence is one of the basic elements in the formulation of an audit methodology (Turley and Cooper, 1991).

Another directly related issue is the process of evaluating and aggregating evidence to support conclusions at different levels and, ultimately, support the final audit opinion. However, not much is known, to date, about the approaches to evidence evaluation that will help in achieving the maximum efficiency and effectiveness of the audit.

The Belief Revision Process

As far as auditing is concerned, evidence is considered the basis on which auditors form their opinion. Spicer and Oppenheim et al. (1990, p. 43) state that:

> The centrality of evidence to the audit is recognised in both the theoretical foundations of auditing and in the practice rules which govern the way audits are carried out. One of the necessary conditions, or theoretical assumptions, of auditing is that there is available sufficient reliable evidence to allow the auditor to form an opinion within reasonable limits of time and cost.

The main focus of auditing studies concerned with evidence has been issues related to sources, types, qualities and sampling of audit evidence (see for example Ricchiute, 1992; Sherer and Kent, 1983; and Spicer and Oppenheim et al., 1990). However, the way auditors approach the collection of evidence and how they integrate pieces of evidence with their current opinions has not received the same attention. Any method of obtaining and evaluating evidence efficiently and effectively would be of great benefit to the audit profession especially with the limited time and cost and increasing work load of accounting firms.

The American auditing literature has focused on the belief revision process or hypothesis updating in evidence evaluation. The focus of auditing researchers on belief revision has been motivated in part by research findings in psychology. These findings suggest that individuals in general follow a belief revision behaviour in seeking to integrate new information with their current beliefs (see for example Hogarth, 1975; Einhorn and Hogarth, 1985; and Edwards, 1968). The belief revision process is mainly a description of the unconscious behaviour followed during information or evidence evaluation. However, a number of benefits might arise from recognising such behaviour and adopting it as an approach in evidence evaluation.

In its auditing context, belief revision assumes that auditors formulate initial beliefs[1] about a client's financial statements and then search for evidence that will allow them to revise their beliefs. The auditors continue to update or revise their beliefs until a final opinion is reached. Anderson (1981, p. 14) stated that:

> In everyday life, information integration is a sequential process. Information is received a piece at a time and integrated into a continuously evolving impression. Each such impression, be it of a theoretical issue, another person, or a social organization, grows and changes over the course of time. At any point in time, therefore, the current impression looks both forward and back.

The audit process involves dealing with uncertainty which makes the formation and revision of beliefs important factors in this process as evidenced from Mock et al. (1997, pp. 123-124):

> ... in an audit context, effectiveness depends on reducing the risk of material misstatement to an acceptably low level. Risk inherently involves uncertainty. Thus, assessing and evaluating uncertainty is an important and inherent feature of the planning and evaluation phases of the audit process. Dealing with uncertainty involves implicitly or explicitly expressing and updating beliefs about uncertain quantities, events or outcomes.

There are indications in the audit literature that the formation and revision of beliefs are of benefit to the audit process. Einhorn (1976) indicated that the formation and revision of beliefs help in structuring the audit. Beliefs, also, help auditors focus evidence search and evaluation, thus making the audit process more tractable (Peters, 1990).

According to the belief revision approach, evidence is classified with respect to the belief under consideration. From this point of view, evidence which auditors gather could be confirming evidence or disconfirming evidence (Church, 1990). Confirming evidence refers to evidence supporting the current belief, while disconfirming evidence refers to evidence denying the belief. Consequently, evidence search strategies could be classified into three strategies; a confirming strategy directed to searching for confirming evidence only, a disconfirming strategy directed

---

[1] Studies in the area of belief revision used the words belief and hypothesis interchangeably. In this study the word belief is used. Chapter 6 includes a discussion about the difference between the two words in the area of belief revision.

toward the search for disconfirming evidence, or a balanced search strategy searching for both confirming and disconfirming evidence.

Ashton et al. (1988) highlighted the importance of future research on auditors' belief formation and revision. As auditors' belief revision is an evolving issue in auditing research, some problems remain unresolved. These problems are related mainly with models employed in measuring belief revision and factors affecting auditors' search for evidence.

The dominant normative model of belief revision is Bayes' theorem. In 1985, Bayes' theorem was superseded by Einhorn and Hogarth's contrast/surprise model (Einhorn and Hogarth, 1985) which has been argued to be more rigorous to the process of belief revision. The Bayesian model describes the decision process as a sequence of multiplicative products of a prior opinion and the diagnosticity of each evidence item. On the other hand, the contrast/surprise model, as a sequential weighting model, describes the decision process as a series of opinion revisions where each revision is the weighted average of the previous judgement and the value of the current evidence item (Pennington and Hastie, 1986).

The contrast/surprise model has been used to investigate the effect of evidence on belief revision. Recent versions of the model are the contrast-inertia model and, most recently, the belief-adjustment model. Auditing studies have focused on the contrast/surprise and belief-adjustment versions of the model.[2] However, the main focus of previous auditing studies was investigating the validity of the predictions of the contrast/surprise model, and its recent version, the belief-adjustment model, in audit settings as the model itself represents a good description of the belief revision process. The interest in the model itself has exceeded the interest in the belief revision approach. In fact, prior auditing research has not systematically studied auditors' attitudes to evidence in belief revision or in any other approach (Bamber et al., 1997).

It is also worth noting that the belief-adjustment model has been focus to other studies in accounting including studies in taxation (Pei et al., 1990) and management accounting (Dillard et al., 1991).

Evidence Evaluation in the UK Auditing Standards

In the US, the belief revision approach is consistent with the American Statement of Auditing Standards No. 56 on analytical procedures (AICPA, 1988). This statement calls for auditors to hypothesise likely causes of unexpected patterns in financial statement balances and to develop plans to investigate. Thus, the statement implies following a belief revision approach by forming an initial belief and then searching for evidence to investigate the plausibility of this belief.

---

[2] As auditing studies focused on the contrast/surprise and belief-adjustment versions of the model, this study will not include the contrast-inertia version of the model. For more details about the contrast-inertia model see Einhorn and Hogarth (1987).

In the UK, audit evidence is governed by Statement of Auditing Standards SAS 400 which provides guidance on the quantity and quality (or reliability) of evidence to be obtained by auditors, and the procedures for obtaining that evidence.

Porter et al. (1996, p. 90) illustrate how SAS 400 relates between audit procedures, audit evidence, and the auditor's opinion. Figure 1.3 shows that audit procedures including compliance (tests of control) and substantive tests are used to gather sufficient and appropriate audit evidence which is used as a basis for the auditor's opinion.

```
Compliance                    Sufficient (quantity)
         \                           \
          > Procedures ────▶ Evidence ────▶ Auditor's opinion
         /                           /
Substantive                   Appropriate (reliable & relevant)
```

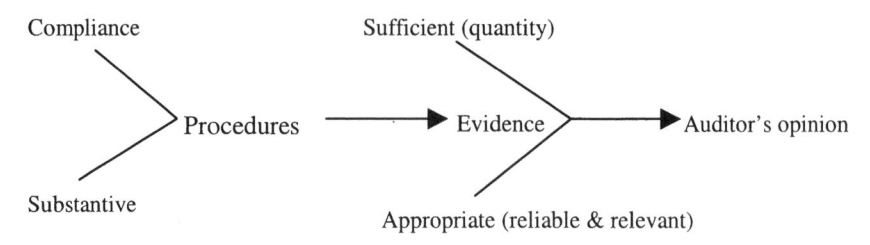

Figure 1.3 Relationship between audit procedures, evidence and the auditor's opinion
Source: Porter et al., 1996, p. 90.

Although SAS 400 makes it clear that audit evidence is obtained through tests of control and substantive tests, there is no explicit mentioning of the belief revision approach, or any other approach. The main statement on audit evidence reads as follows:

Auditors should obtain sufficient appropriate audit evidence to be able to draw reasonable conclusions on which to base the audit opinion (APB, 1995, SAS 400.1).

The statement does not imply following a specific approach in searching for evidence. It only indicates that evidence obtained should be sufficient and appropriate. Audit evidence is obtained through tests of control and substantive procedures. The statement on tests of control states that:

In seeking to obtain audit evidence from tests of control, auditors should consider the sufficiency and appropriateness of the audit evidence to support the assessed level of control risk (APB, 1995, SAS 400.2).

The above statement is more specific and provides some insight about the evidence search and evaluation approach. According to the statement evidence should be obtained to support the assessed level of control risk. This implies starting with the assessed level of control risk as an initial belief and then searching for evidence to support or deny this level.

The statement on substantive procedures states that:

In seeking to obtain audit evidence from substantive procedures, auditors should consider the extent to which that evidence together with any evidence from tests of controls supports the relevant financial statement assertions (APB, 1995, SAS 400.3).

Unlike evidence from tests of controls, the statement on substantive procedures implies starting with the financial statement assertions as the initial belief and then searching for evidence to support or deny these assertions.

The Statement of Auditing Standards on audit planning (APB, 1995, SAS 200) does not state anything about forming initial beliefs. However, the explanations provided indicate that planning the audit work helps in ensuring that potential problems are identified.

It is also relevant to consider the UK statement on investigating fluctuations or unexpected relationships which states that:

When significant fluctuations or unexpected relationships are identified that are inconsistent with other relevant information or that deviate from predicted patterns, auditors should investigate and obtain adequate explanations and appropriate corroborative evidence (APB, 1995, SAS 410.4).

Unlike the American SAS 56, the UK SAS 410.4 implies following an open-minded approach rather than a belief revision one in searching for and evaluation of audit evidence. However, it should be noted that employing analytical review techniques would at some stage involve forming initial beliefs in the form of anticipated results to be compared with actual information (Millichamp, 1990).

In conducting an analytical review the auditor would predict the expected result. The difference between this predicted result and the actual result would determine the extent of substantive tests and other investigations needed (Hatherly, 1980). Therefore, one can conclude that analytical review procedures involve forming an initial belief in the form of anticipation or prediction of expected results. However, the initial beliefs, as indicated by the American SAS 56, have a different meaning. They refer to forming expectations about the likely causes of fluctuations in the financial statements. Up to date, there is no empirical evidence to support the formation of this form of beliefs in the audit practice.

Aims of the Study

Given the different approaches taken by the US and UK standards, one might question whether this is reflected in auditor decision-making behaviour in those countries. Previous auditing studies in the US assumed that auditors follow a belief revision approach. However, there is insufficient evidence to support that this is a general practice as previous studies did not directly investigate this issue.

Motivated by the research findings in the area of belief revision, the aim of this study is to investigate whether auditors follow a belief revision approach in their evaluation of evidence, and the appropriateness of such an approach in audit settings. The study aims also at finding out the effect of following a belief revision approach on the efficiency and effectiveness of the audit process.

Research Questions

The previous auditing studies did not address the question of whether the belief revision approach is followed by auditors in their evaluation of evidence. The failure to address this issue together with the fact that the UK auditing standards do not provide specific guidelines about the evidence evaluation approach means that we do not have a clear idea of the audit practice concerning evidence search and evaluation. This leads to the following main research question:

1. *Do auditors in practice follow a belief revision approach in their evaluation of evidence?*

The main variables included in the belief revision approach, and hence in the belief-adjustment model, are the initial belief and new pieces of confirming and disconfirming evidence. Many factors will affect the formation of the initial belief and the way auditors approach pieces of confirming and disconfirming evidence and assign weight to them. The need for further empirical support to the findings of previous studies are reasons for developing the following research question:

2. *What are the factors that affect auditors' evaluation of evidence and, in particular what are the factors affecting the formation of the initial beliefs and the weight assigned to different pieces of evidence?*

The belief revision approach is claimed to be of benefit to the efficiency and effectiveness of the audit process. As the belief is updated after receiving new pieces of evidence, this helps keeping a running total and reducing the memory load.

> From a cognitive viewpoint, the advantage of an anchoring-and-adjustment strategy is that it allows one to keep a 'running total' of the effects of prior information while reducing memory load (Einhorn and Hogarth, 1985, p. 5).

Consequently, this will reduce the time consumed to arrive at a final opinion. Hence, the following research question is developed:

3. *Are there any benefits from following a belief revision approach in auditing particularly benefits related to improving the efficiency and effectiveness of the audit process?*

Structure of the Book

To achieve the aims of the study and address the research questions, the study is organised as follows.

Chapter 2 discusses the belief revision approach and the belief-adjustment model, and its earlier version, the contrast/surprise model. The forms of both versions of the model and their predictions are presented. This is followed by a discussion of the reasons for focusing on the belief-adjustment model in audit settings. The last section of chapter 2 analyses the previous auditing studies that investigated the validity of the predictions of both versions of the model and their main findings.

In chapter 3, factors that affect the belief revision approach are discussed. Each factor is discussed and the findings of previous studies concerning its implications are presented.

The review of the literature in chapters 2 and 3 serves two purposes. First, it helps in providing an insight of the belief revision approach with relation to the initial belief and how it is updated with subsequent pieces of evidence. Second, the review of the previous literature will help in the design and direction of the empirical study. Factors considered by the previous studies with relation to the belief revision approach will be investigated. Besides, the empirical study will also address aspects of the belief revision approach that were not addressed by the previous studies.

Chapter 4 presents the research design of this study. The study depends on two research methods; interviews and experiments. Interviews are employed to explore the extent of practice of the belief revision approach. The results of the interviews together with the results of previous studies will help in determining the design of the subsequent experimental study. The main aim of the experimental study will be to find out the benefits of employing the belief revision approach in auditing.

In chapters 5 and 6, the results of the interviews are presented and analysed with the aim to provide an insight of the process of evidence evaluation.

Chapter 7 will present the results of the experimental study with the aim to draw a conclusion on whether there are any benefits from employing the belief revision approach in audit evidence evaluation.

Chapter 8 is a conclusion and discussion of the main results and areas for future research.

Chapter 2

The Belief-Adjustment as a Model of the Belief Revision Approach

Introduction

Auditing studies in the area of belief revision addressed issues that either related to the belief-adjustment model or to the factors affecting auditors' formation of the initial beliefs and their attitudes toward pieces of evidence. This chapter is concerned with studies that focused on the belief-adjustment model, and its earlier version, the contrast/surprise model. The discussion of the results of these studies will help in providing a better understanding of belief revision as the model itself is a good representation of such behaviour.

The following points are addressed in this chapter:
- The contrast/surprise model and its predictions.
- The belief-adjustment model and its predictions.
- Advantages of the belief-adjustment model.
- The validity of the contrast/surprise and belief-adjustment model predictions.

The Contrast/Surprise Model and its Predictions

The contrast/surprise model was introduced by Einhorn and Hogarth (1985) to measure the strength of a belief after incorporating new pieces of evidence. According to the model the strength of the current belief is equal to the strength of the initial belief updated by the weight of new pieces of evidence. The contrast/surprise model takes into consideration the following factors:
- **Evidence direction.** Evidence gathered could be positive or negative. In an auditing context, positive evidence is evidence indicating favourable characteristics of a client or financial statements, while negative evidence is evidence indicating unfavourable characteristics. Positive evidence could be confirming or disconfirming depending on the initial belief. The same applies to negative evidence.[1]

---

[1] Einhorn and Hogarth (1985) and Hogarth and Einhorn (1992) used the words positive and confirming interchangeably to refer to evidence supporting a belief. They also used the words negative and disconfirming interchangeably to refer to evidence denying a belief. In the current study, evidence is classified to positive and negative with respect to the

14   *Behavioural Aspects of Auditors' Evidence Evaluation*

- **Evidence strength.** Evidence strength refers to the degree to which a piece of evidence confirms or disconfirms a belief.
- **Evidence type.** Evidence gathered could be all of the same direction (e.g. positive evidence) or it could be mixed evidence.
- **Evidence order.** Weak evidence could follow strong evidence, or vice versa, and disconfirming evidence could follow confirming evidence, or vice versa.
- **Response or evaluation mode.** Evidence can be evaluated step-by-step (SbS) or at the end-of-sequence (EoS). In the SbS mode, evidence is evaluated one at a time as soon as each piece is received. In the EoS mode, evidence is evaluated altogether after receiving all the pieces.

The contrast/surprise model is based on a discounting model for discounting the strength of beliefs on the basis of disconfirming evidence, and an accretion model for confirming evidence (Einhorn and Hogarth, 1985). For mixed evidence, both the discounting model and the accretion model are used. The algebraic formula of the contrast/surprise model and its predictions are as follows.

When disconfirming pieces of evidence are evaluated and used to update the current belief, the following formula called the discounting model is used:
$S_k = S_{k-1} - S_{k-1} a_k^{\alpha}$
However, when confirming pieces of evidence are evaluated and used to update the current belief, a different formula, called the accretion model, is used.
$S_k = S_{k-1} + (1 - S_{k-1}) b_k^{\beta}$
where,
S_k = strength of belief after evaluating k pieces of evidence ($0 \leq S_k \leq 1$).
S_{k-1} = the initial strength of the belief before evaluating the kth piece of evidence ($0 \leq S_{k-1} \leq 1$).
a_k^{α} = the subjective strength of the kth piece of disconfirming evidence where α (≥ 0) represents an individual's attitude toward disconfirming evidence ($0 \leq a_k^{\alpha} \leq 1$).
b_k^{β} = the subjective strength of the kth piece of confirming evidence where β (≥ 0) represents an individual's attitude toward confirming evidence ($0 \leq b_k^{\beta} \leq 1$).
The mixed evidence model is simply the previous two models together.
$S_k = S_{k-1} - S_{k-1} a_k^{\alpha}$ (for disconfirming evidence)
$S_k = S_{k-1} + (1 - S_{k-1}) b_k^{\beta}$ (for confirming evidence)

The contrast/surprise model predicts that for consistent confirming or disconfirming evidence there are no order effects. In other words, the order by which pieces of consistent evidence are evaluated has no effect on the strength of the final belief. Furthermore, no order effects occur even if the consistent pieces of evidence differ in their strength. For example, if an auditor believes initially that debtors are likely to be materially correct by 85%, and if subsequently the auditor gets two pieces of disconfirming evidence x and z (which are at the same time negative evidence). The auditor assigns a 35% subjective strength for x, and a 75% subjective strength for z. Assuming α and β each equals 1, the strength of the auditor's belief after evaluating

---

characteristics of a client or financial statements. On the other hand, evidence is classified to confirming or disconfirming with respect to the belief under consideration.

the two pieces of evidence is calculated according to the contrast/surprise model as follows:
$S_2 = 0.85 (1 - 0.35) (1 - 0.75) = 0.14$
Since multiplication is commutative, S_2 is not affected by the order of the two pieces of evidence. The same applies to consistent confirming evidence. It is also noticed that since the initial belief was relatively strong (85%), the disconfirming evidence had a great effect on it. This is what Einhorn and Hogarth (1985) refer to as the 'contrast' or 'surprise' effect.

However, if the auditor gathers two pieces of mixed evidence, one confirming and the other disconfirming, the order in which these two pieces of evidence are evaluated will have an effect on the strength of the final belief when evidence is evaluated in a SbS mode. If for example an auditor initially believes that debtors are materially correct by 60%, and then s/he gets one piece of confirming evidence and assigns a 80% subjective weight to it. Afterwards, s/he gets a disconfirming piece of evidence and assigns a 70% subjective weight to it. According to the contrast/surprise model, and assuming α and β each equals 1, the strength of the final belief is calculated as follows.
First for the confirming piece of evidence, the accretion model is used.
$S_1 = 0.60 + (1 - 0.60)(0.80) = 0.92$
The 0.92 is then taken as the anchor for the next piece of disconfirming evidence and the discounting model is used.
$S_1 = 0.92 (1 - 0.70) = 0.28$

This means that after evaluating the two pieces of mixed evidence the auditor would believe that the debtors are materially correct by only 28%. If, however, the two pieces of evidence were received in a disconfirming/confirming order, the calculations would be as follows.
First, for the disconfirming piece of evidence, the discounting model is used.
$S_1 = 0.60 (1 - 0.70) = 0.18$
Then the accretion model is used for the confirming piece of evidence with 0.18 as the prior belief.
$S_1 = 0.18 + (1 - 0.18)(0.80) = 0.84$

In the latter case, the final belief of the auditor is that debtors are materially correct by 84%. It is noticed that there is a significant difference between this situation and the situation where the same two pieces of evidence were evaluated in a confirming/disconfirming order and the final belief was 28%. This implies that order might significantly affect the final opinion. In auditing, this conclusion might have significant practical implications.

The Belief-Adjustment Model and its Predictions

The belief-adjustment model is the most recent version of the contrast/surprise model. In the belief-adjustment model it is assumed that '... people handle belief-updating tasks by a general, sequential anchoring-and-adjustment process in which current opinion, or the anchor, is adjusted by the impact of succeeding pieces of evidence' (Hogarth and Einhorn, 1992, p. 8). Thus, the aim of the belief-adjustment model is still the same as the contrast/surprise model; measuring the strength of a belief after incorporating the effect of new pieces of evidence. Hogarth and Einhorn (1992, p. 2) describe the belief-adjustment model as 'a descriptive theory of belief updating that can be applied to many substantive domains'.

The belief-adjustment model takes into consideration more factors than the contrast/surprise model. Besides evidence direction, strength, type, order and response mode, the belief-adjustment model considers the type of task, and length and complexity of evidence. The model differentiates between estimation and evaluation tasks. The belief-adjustment model predicts that estimation-type tasks, like audit planning decisions, will produce data which fits nonadditive averaging integration models. This means that pieces of evidence are integrated by getting the *average* of their values. On the other hand, evaluation-type tasks, like evaluating internal control systems, will produce data which fits additive summation integration models. This means that pieces of evidence are integrated by getting the *sum* of their values (Kerr and Ward, 1994).

According to the length of evidence, Hogarth and Einhorn (1992) indicate that short series of evidence refers to evidence between 2 and 12 items, while long series refers to evidence of 17 or more items. According to the complexity of evidence, Hogarth and Einhorn (1992) consider evidence to be simple if it involves a single item of information in tasks with which one could be reasonably familiar. On the other hand, a piece of evidence is considered to be complex if it involves a large amount of information or unfamiliar tasks. Thus, it is not only the complexity of information, but also the familiarity with and knowledge of the task which will determine the degree of complexity of evidence.

The general algebraic formula of the belief-adjustment model is as follows (Hogarth and Einhorn, 1992):

$$S_k = S_{k-1} + w_k[s(x_k) - R]$$

where

S_k = degree of belief in some hypothesis, impression or attitude after evaluating k pieces of evidence ($0 \leq S_k \leq 1$).

S_{k-1} = anchor or prior opinion. The initial strength of belief is denoted S_0.

$s(x_k)$ = subjective evaluation of the kth piece of evidence. (Different people may accord the same evidence, x_k, different evaluations).

R = the reference point or background against which the impact of the kth piece of evidence is evaluated.

w_k = the adjustment weight for the kth piece of evidence ($0 \leq w_k \leq 1$).

The general formula of the model varies according to the type of task, response mode and adjustment weight of evidence. Hogarth and Einhorn (1992) argue that in evaluation-type tasks evidence is encoded as confirming or disconfirming relative to the belief under consideration irrespective of the level of this belief. This means that confirming evidence increases the belief while disconfirming evidence decreases it. In this case, the reference point R = 0, and the model takes the following form:

$S_k = S_{k-1} + w_k s(x_k)$

However, in estimation-type tasks, evidence is encoded with respect to the level of the current belief. In this case, the reference point R = the level of the current belief S_{k-1}, and the model takes the following form:

$S_k = S_{k-1} + w_k[s(x_k) - S_{k-1}]$

To illustrate the difference between evaluation and estimation tasks, Hogarth and Einhorn (1992, p. 10) provided the following example. Assume that the current opinion or belief is .5 and that two pieces of confirming evidence were gathered. If the task is an evaluation-type task, evidence is evaluated irrespective of the level of the current belief. In this case, let the evidence items have values of +.7 and +.3, respectively. This means that the level of the current belief will increase after receiving the new pieces of evidence whether they are received in a strong-weak or weak-strong order. The reason for this is that in evaluation-type tasks the value of each piece of evidence is added to the level of the current belief. Therefore, any confirming evidence will increase the level of the current belief and any disconfirming evidence will decrease it.

However, if the task is an estimation-type task, evidence is evaluated with respect to the level of the current belief. In this case, let the evidence items have values of .9 and .6, respectively. The level of the current belief (.5) is adjusted after each piece of evidence through an averaging process and not a summation one. Thus, if the evidence is received in a strong-weak order, the level of the current belief will increase after the first piece of evidence because .9 > .5, then it will decrease after the second piece because .6 < the average of .9 and .5. However, if evidence is received in a weak-strong order, there will be an increase in the level of the belief after both pieces of evidence because .6 > .5 and .9 > the average of .6 and .5.

According to the response mode, the general formula of the model represents a SbS mode as it is more likely to be used by people when integrating new evidence with current beliefs (Hogarth and Einhorn, 1992). However, if an EoS mode is adopted, the formula of the model would be as follows:

$S_k = S_0 + w_k[s(x_1, \ldots, x_k) - R]$

With respect to the adjustment weight w_k, Hogarth and Einhorn (1992) argue that it depends on the sign of the impact of the evidence, $[s(x_k) - R]$, and the level of the anchor, S_{k-1}. If the subjective strength of the evidence $s(x_k) \leq$ the reference point R, then the adjustment weight is proportional to S_{k-1}, and the model takes the following form:

$S_k = S_{k-1} + \alpha\, S_{k-1}[s(x_k) - R]$

where α is the individual's sensitivity toward disconfirming evidence and $0 \leq \alpha \leq 1$

However, if the subjective strength of the evidence $s(x_k) >$ the reference point R, the model takes the following form:

$S_k = S_{k-1} + \beta\,(1 - S_{k-1})\,[s(x_k) - R]$

where β is the individual's sensitivity toward confirming evidence and $0 \leq \beta \leq 1$

The belief-adjustment model is more complicated and takes into consideration more factors than the contrast/surprise model. Accordingly, the predictions of the belief-adjustment model are more complicated depending on the various factors incorporated into the model. However, the model still predicts order effects as in the contrast/surprise model. The same example of the auditor who initially believes that debtors are materially correct by 60% is used for illustration. The auditor first gets a confirming evidence and assigns 80% subjective weight to it. As this is assumed to be a SbS mode, then the reference point R = 0, and the current belief is calculated as follows.

$S_1 = 0.60 + (1 - 0.60)(0.80) = 0.92$

Afterwards, the auditor gets a disconfirming piece of evidence and assigns a 70% subjective weight to it. The strength of the auditor's belief after this disconfirming piece of evidence is calculated as follows:

$S_1 = 0.92 + (0.92)(-0.70) = 0.28$

However, if the auditor receives the evidence in a disconfirming/confirming order, the calculations are as follows:

$S_1 = 0.60 + (0.60)(-0.70) = 0.18$
$S_1 = 0.18 + (1 - 0.18)(0.80) = 0.84$

The calculations of the belief-adjustment model are identical to those of the contrast/surprise model. The change in the strength of the final belief as a result of the change of evidence order from confirming/disconfirming to disconfirming/confirming is clearly significant and might result in serious effects on the auditor's report. The complete predictions of the belief-adjustment model regarding order effects are presented in table 2.1.

Table 2.1 Order effect predictions of the belief-adjustment model

Task Type	Estimation		Evaluation			
Evidence Type	All		Mixed		Consistent	
Response Mode	EoS	SbS	EoS	SbS	EoS	SbS
Short Series						
Simple	Primacy	Recency	Primacy	Recency	Primacy	No effect
Complex	Recency	Recency	Recency	Recency	No effect	No effect
Long Series	Force toward primacy	Force toward primacy	Force toward primacy	Force toward primacy	Primacy	Primacy

Source: Hogarth and Einhorn, 1992, p. 17.

Table 2.1 shows that the predictions of the model depend on the type of the task to be performed. For estimation-type tasks, the predictions of the model are the same for both mixed and consistent evidence. For evaluation-type tasks, the predictions of the model differ according to the consistency of evidence. The predictions of the model for both estimation and evaluation tasks depend also on the response mode, and length and complexity of evidence.

There are two types of order effects; primacy and recency effects. A primacy effect means that the first piece (or few pieces) of evidence has the greatest impact on the belief. A recency effect, on the other hand, means that the last piece (or few pieces) of evidence has the greatest impact on the belief.

For estimation-type tasks, the model predicts a primacy effect for short series of simple evidence processed at an EoS response mode. However, there is a recency effect for short series of simple evidence in the SbS response mode, and for short series of complex evidence in both response modes. For long series of evidence there is a force toward primacy in both response modes.

In evaluation-type tasks, the predictions of the model differ according to the type of evidence; mixed or consistent. For mixed evidence, the predictions are exactly the same as estimation-type tasks. For consistent evidence, the model predicts a primacy effect for short series of simple evidence in the EoS response mode, and for long series of evidence in both response modes. However, no effect was predicted for short series of simple evidence in the SbS response mode and for short series of complex evidence in both response modes.

Advantages of the Belief-Adjustment Model

Auditing studies have started to focus on the belief-adjustment model as it reflects the belief revision approach of incorporating new evidence with current beliefs. Previous auditing studies focused mainly on investigating the model's predictions. The model has been regarded by auditing researchers as a convenient descriptive model of auditors' decision-making. Hogarth and Einhorn's belief-adjustment model attempts to understand how separate pieces of information are accounted for in formulating decisions (Moeckel, 1991).

The belief-adjustment model has been employed for research purposes for two main reasons. First, the model takes into consideration different task characteristics, information-processing strategies, and modes of encoding, i.e. whether an averaging or a summation model is employed (Tubbs et al., 1993). The second reason for employing the belief-adjustment model is that one criterion of any model is for it to be operational for research purposes and to reflect the process it represents. The audit process as it has been described by Mautz and Sharaf (1961) is a multistage task where auditors accept a certain problem which is the audit itself, decompose it into a set of hypotheses, take a tentative position on each, iterate through a set of tests and revisions of the hypotheses, make judgements, and then consider all this work together to arrive at a composite judgement.

Another description of the audit process, yet not a different one, is that provided by Messier and Plumlee (1987). They describe auditing as a sequential anchoring-and-adjustment process where the development of the preliminary audit plan is based upon the auditor's beliefs about the client's internal control system. These beliefs are formed during the preliminary orientation and initial evaluation of internal controls. The audit plan outlines the mix of tests that the auditor believes to be the most efficient and effective under the circumstances, and may be revised if evidence obtained in subsequent tests indicates that the auditor's initial beliefs were inaccurate.

Messier and Plumlee (1987) add that evidence obtained from each audit procedure provides information about the condition of the client's accounting system and account balances and, consequently, about the accuracy of the auditor's beliefs. However, up to date, no studies address directly the issue of locating the position of the initial beliefs in the audit process and the timing when the auditor starts to form these beliefs.

Christ (1993) argues that the auditor forms *expectations* about the likelihood of errors in the financial statements which will help in developing the audit strategy. Christ suggested a framework of the audit planning task to show how these expectations are embodied in the auditor's problem representation. This framework provides some insight about the timing when the auditor starts to form the initial beliefs. Figure 2.1 illustrates Christ's framework of the audit planning process. As the various planning tasks are completed, the auditor will internally develop a representation of the problem in the form of expectations about the likelihood of errors in the financial statements. This problem representation is then integrated with the available information which will help in developing the audit strategy about the planned tests of controls and substantive tests.

Even though not much is known about auditors' formation of initial beliefs, the description of the audit process as a multistage task or a sequential anchoring-and-adjustment process supports employing the belief-adjustment model in studies that address issues related to auditors' evidence evaluation. The importance of such studies arises from the fact that the manner in which evidence is evaluated and integrated with prior beliefs and with other evidence could have a very practical effect on audit judgements and subsequent actions (Kerr and Ward, 1994). Kerr and Ward (1994) add that the belief-adjustment model provides specific predictions concerning the effects of the judgement task on evidence integration. The fashion in which auditors integrate evidence has potential implications for the effectiveness and efficiency of the audit. Effectiveness can be affected since the combination rule used to integrate evidence may influence the auditor's beliefs and subsequent actions, with a corresponding impact on achieved detection risk. From an efficiency perspective, different combination rules can lead to different judgements concerning the appropriate extent of testing.

In a study by Biggs and Mock (1983) they concluded that auditors who followed a directed strategy consisting of selecting a particular audit step and then searching for information relevant to that step were more efficient than auditors who performed the task depending on a thorough and sequential search of available information before making any decisions. The directed strategy referred to in Biggs and Mock's study is similar to a great extent to the belief revision approach. In a study by Messier and Plumlee (1987), although it did not directly refer to the belief revision approach, the results pointed out that anticipation or auditor's beliefs about the client's internal control system are more likely to reduce the amount of planned work. A good example of this conclusion is that given by Messier and Plumlee (1987, p. 350) as follows:

The Belief-Adjustment Model   21

Audit Planning Subtasks
- Obtain client background information
- Set materiality level
- Perform preliminary analytical review
- Assess inherent risk
- Understand internal control structure
- Assess control control risk
- Determine detection risk

Audit Planning Knowledge Strucure (Internal)

Knowledge Retrieval (Internal) and Information Search (External)

Available Information (External)

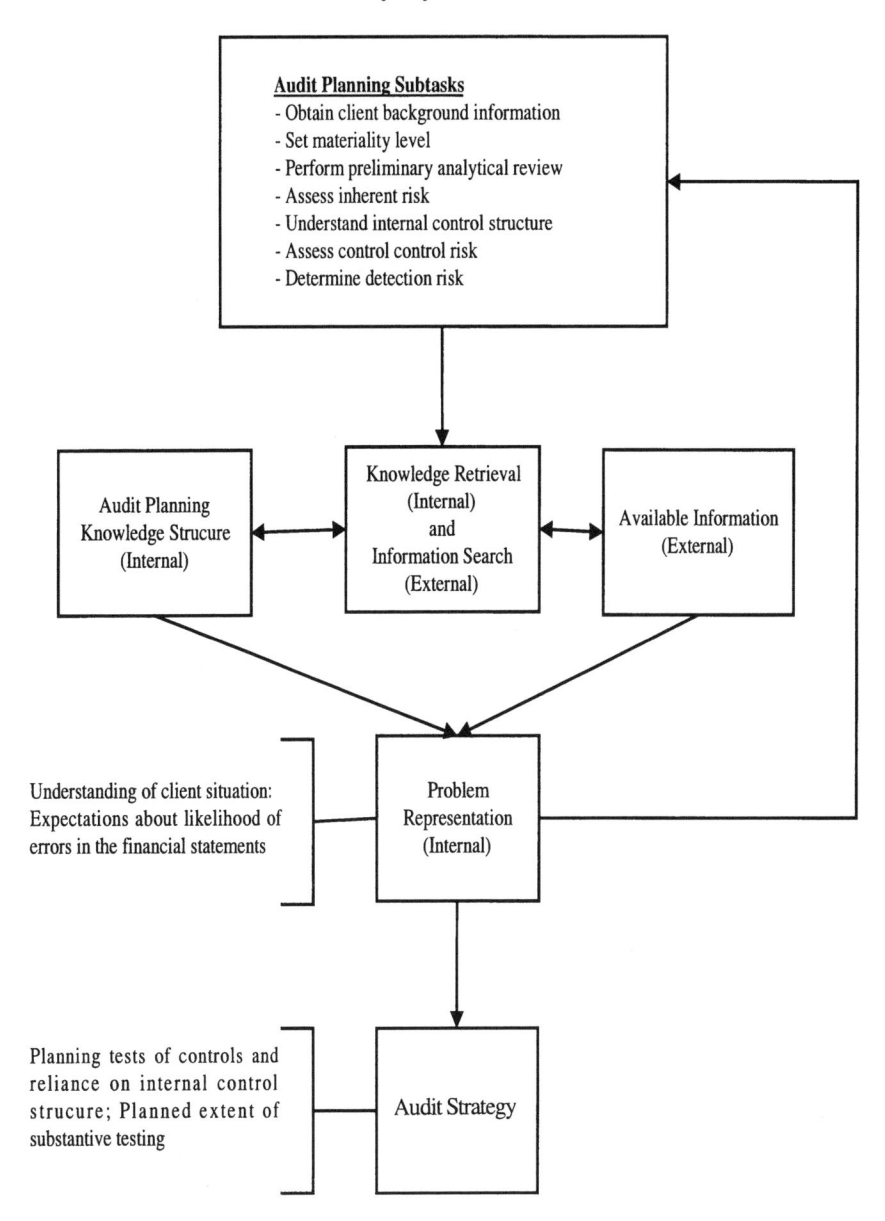

Understanding of client situation: Expectations about likelihood of errors in the financial statements

Problem Representation (Internal)

Planning tests of controls and reliance on internal control strucure; Planned extent of substantive testing

Audit Strategy

Figure 2.1 The audit planning task
Source: Christ, 1993, p. 307.

... an auditor who reviews an accounting control system and conducts compliance tests may conclude that sales with unauthorized sales terms are likely to have occurred. The auditor 'anticipates' finding evidence of unauthorized sales terms in substantive test results. The audit plan would incorporate tests to determine the effect on the account balances of unauthorized sales terms. Then, if the anticipated audit evidence were found in substantive test, no revision of the audit plan would occur because the appropriate tests were already incorporated in the plan. On the other hand, an auditor who had evaluated the same system without anticipating sales with unauthorized sales terms would not have incorporated procedures in the audit plan. Finding evidence of unauthorized sales terms in substantive tests should lead this auditor to revise the audit plan since the current plan would not have specifically addressed such unanticipated problems.

However, Felix and Kinney (1982) claim that not much is known about the way auditors integrate information or evidence from compliance and substantive tests.

Although the previous discussion indicates the suitability of employing the belief-adjustment model in auditing research, Bamber et al. (1997) argue that auditing research in the area of belief revision employs the belief-adjustment model as the 'assumed model' of belief revision, and does not comprehensively address the model's descriptive validity. Bamber et al. (1997) conducted numerous analyses to test the descriptive validity of the belief-adjustment as a model of the belief revision approach in evidence evaluation. The results provided strong support for the descriptive validity of the model. However, Bamber et al. (1997) did not address the issue of whether the belief revision approach itself is employed by auditors in practice.

The Validity of the Predictions of the Contrast/Surprise and Belief-Adjustment Models

Auditing studies that investigated the validity of the predictions of the contrast/surprise model and the belief-adjustment model focused mainly on the order effect predictions. The results of almost all the previous auditing studies were consistent with part of the predictions of both versions of the model. Although these previous studies depended on laboratory experiments in audit settings to test for the presence of order effects, the studies provide a better understanding of aspects of the belief revision approach including:
- Audit tasks in which a belief revision approach could be employed.
- The way auditors revise their beliefs with subsequent pieces of evidence to arrive at an opinion.
- Factors that might affect auditors' decision-making in evidence evaluation including evidence order and evaluation mode, belief frame, and experience.

The Validity of the Predictions of the Contrast/Surprise Model in Auditing

The contrast/surprise model predicts a recency effect for mixed evidence in the SbS mode and no order effects for consistent evidence. However, the model did not differentiate in its predictions between evaluation and estimation-type tasks. Rather, the predictions were the same as the predictions of the belief-adjustment model in the case of evaluation-type tasks and short series of simple evidence.

A summary of the studies that investigated the validity of the predictions of the contrast/surprise model is presented in table 2.2 showing the variables included in each study and its main findings.

Evaluating internal controls over payroll is an evaluation-type task used by Ashton and Ashton (1988) to test for recency effects. The investigation was carried out by three experiments, two of which subjects were presented with four pieces of simple consistent evidence (positive and negative evidence respectively). The third experiment involved four mixed pieces of simple evidence; two pieces of positive and two pieces of negative evidence. The three experiments were carried out in a SbS mode. The results of these experiments were consistent with the predictions of the contrast/surprise model; no order effects for consistent evidence and recency effects for mixed evidence.

Another internal control evaluation task is that of evaluating the internal controls over the sales-debtors-collection cycle. Ashton and Ashton (1988) employed this task to test also for recency effects. However, unlike evaluating internal controls over payroll, they conducted only one experiment where subjects were presented with mixed evidence. Subjects were asked to evaluate two pieces of simple positive evidence and two pieces of simple negative evidence in a SbS mode. The results supported the presence of recency effects.

Butt and Campbell (1989) conducted their study to test for recency effects in case of evaluating the internal control system in general. The study involved one experiment where subjects were presented with general facts about the internal controls and no specific controls were mentioned. Unlike Ashton and Ashton (1988), the study depended on ten pieces of evidence, five positive and five negative. Butt and Campbell did not indicate clearly whether they employed a SbS mode or an EoS one in conducting their study. They stated that subjects were asked to give their evaluation of each set of five pieces of evidence together. This situation could not be viewed as a SbS or an EoS mode. Rather, it is a combination of the two. The results of the study supported part of the predictions of the contrast/surprise model. Recency effects existed only when subjects started with low prior beliefs. Low prior beliefs referred to negative beliefs about the internal control system. When subjects started with positive or high prior beliefs about the internal control system, no significant order effects were found.

Table 2.2 Summary of auditing studies on the contrast/surprise model

Study	Experiment	Type of Task			Type of Evidence		Length of Evidence		Complexity of Evidence		Response Mode		Main Results
		Estimation	Evaluation	Consistent	Mixed		Short	Long	Simple	Complex	EoS	SbS	
Ashton & Ashton, 1988	1,2	-	✓	✓	-		✓	-	✓	-	-	✓	No Effect
	3,4	-	✓	-	✓		✓	-	✓	-	-	✓	Recency
	5	-	✓	✓	-		✓	-	✓	-	✓	✓	Response mode has an effect
Butt & Campbell, 1989	1	-	✓	-	✓		✓	-	•	•	•	•	Recency with low prior beliefs

✓ Investigated by study or experiment
- Not investigated by study or experiment
• Study did not differentiate between types included in this variable

A different evaluation-type task is that of evaluating the debtors balance. Ashton and Ashton (1988) employed this task to examine the effect of the response mode on auditors' beliefs in case of consistent evidence. Four pieces of simple positive evidence were presented to one group of subjects, while the other group was presented with four pieces of negative evidence. Both SbS and EoS modes were manipulated. The result indicated less extreme belief revisions with EoS than with SbS mode. This result implies that auditors are evidence prone. In other words, auditors are willing to revise their beliefs with new pieces of evidence.

The Validity of the Predictions of the Belief-Adjustment Model in Auditing

The predictions of the belief-adjustment model are based on the type of task. Hogarth and Einhorn (1992) differentiated between estimation and evaluation tasks. The significant difference between the two types of tasks is that with estimation tasks order effects occur with mixed and consistent evidence, whereas with evaluation-type tasks order effects are more evident for mixed evidence. Most auditing studies that investigated the validity of the model's predictions employed evaluation-type tasks. Table 2.3 presents a summary of the auditing studies that investigated the validity of the belief-adjustment model predictions including the variables in each study and the main results.

The task of evaluating internal control effectiveness for the sales-debtors cycle was used by Kerr and Ward (1994) as part of their study. However, Kerr and Ward's study did not address the recency effect predictions. It addressed the predictions of the belief-adjustment model concerning the relationship between the type of task and evidence integration models, an issue that has not received a great deal of concern. The results supported the predictions of the model that evaluation-type tasks will result in judgements that fit summation integration models.

Trotman and Wright (1996) also employed the task of evaluating the internal controls in their study. However, unlike Kerr and Ward (1994), they aimed at investigating the presence of recency effects. Trotman and Wright (1996) conducted an experiment in which audit managers, seniors, and students were asked to complete the task of evaluating the internal controls over the debtors. The subjects were presented with four pieces of mixed evidence and both evidence evaluation modes were manipulated (SbS and EoS). The results indicated the presence of recency effects. However, experience affected these recency effects. Students displayed recency in both evidence evaluation modes. Seniors displayed a marginal recency in the SbS mode only, while managers did not display any significant recency effects. These results indicate that recency effects are mitigated by experience. Evidence evaluation mode might also have an effect on recency as evidenced from the seniors' results. However, this latter issue was not discussed in the study.

Table 2.3 Summary of auditing studies on the belief-adjustment model

Study	Experiment	Type of Task Estimation	Type of Task Evaluation	Type of Evidence Consistent	Type of Evidence Mixed	Length of Evidence Short	Length of Evidence Long	Complexity of Evidence Simple	Complexity of Evidence Complex	Response Mode EoS	Response Mode SbS	Main Results
Tubbs et al., 1990	1,2	-	✓	✓	-	✓	-	-	✓	✓	✓	No Effect
	3	-	✓	-	✓	✓	-	-	✓	✓	✓	Order in SbS
	4	-	✓	-	✓	✓	-	-	✓	✓	✓	Order in EoS & SbS
Messier, 1992	1,2	-	✓	-	✓	✓	-	-	✓	-	✓	Recency but did not lead to different actions
Asare, 1992	1	-	✓	-	✓	✓	-	•	•	-	✓	Recency even with different belief frames
Pei et al., 1992	1	-	✓	-	✓	✓	-	•	•	-	✓	Recency
Krull et al., 1993	1	-	✓	-	✓	✓	-	•	•	-	✓	More recency with experience
Kennedy, 1993	1	-	✓	-	✓	✓	-	✓	✓	✓	-	Accountability and experience mitigated recency
Messier & Tubbs, 1994	1	-	✓	-	✓	✓	-	-	✓	•	•	Recency but mitigated by experience

Table 2.3 (continued)

Study	Experiment	Type of Task		Type of Evidence			Length of Evidence		Complexity of Evidence		Response Mode		Main Results
		Estimation	Evaluation	Consistent	Mixed	Short	Long	Simple	Complex	EoS	SbS	
Kerr & Ward, 1994	1	-	✓	-	✓	•	•	•	•	•	•	Evaluation tasks fit summation models & Estimation tasks fit averaging models
	2	✓	-	-	✓	•	•	•	•	•	•	
Trotman & Wright, 1996	1	-	✓	-	✓	✓	-	✓	-	✓	✓	Recency
	2	-	✓	-	✓	✓	-	✓	✓	✓	✓	Experience mitigated recency
Cushing & Ahlawat, 1996	1	-	✓	-	✓	✓	-	-	✓	-	✓	Documentation mitigated recency

✓ Investigated by study or experiment
- Not investigated by study or experiment
• Study did not differentiate between types included in this variable

A debtors scenario evaluation-type task was used by Tubbs et al. (1990) as their study involved a task dealing with the likelihood of collection from a major client. Order effects were tested for in case of consistent positive and negative evidence, and in case of mixed evidence. Both EoS and SbS modes were manipulated. The results indicated no significant order effects for consistent evidence whether it was positive or negative, while a recency effect occurred in the case of mixed evidence. However, recency effects in case of using two pieces of mixed evidence occurred only in the SbS mode. In case of using four pieces of mixed evidence, recency occurred in both the EoS and SbS modes. The same debtors scenario was used again by Messier and Tubbs (1994) with four pieces of mixed evidence evaluated in an EoS mode. However, they aimed at testing the effect of experience on recency effects and concluded that less experienced auditors showed significantly greater recency than more experienced auditors. This result is consistent with the findings of Trotman and Wright (1996) that experience mitigated recency effects.

Auditing the creditors is also an evaluation-type task that has been investigated. Tubbs et al. (1990) employed a task involving the evaluation of a potential understatement of liabilities in the form of a creditors scenario dealing with the likelihood that creditors are fairly stated. Order of evidence was manipulated by including consistent positive and consistent negative evidence in two experiments in either a stronger/weaker or weaker/stronger order. Mixed evidence was also used in two experiments in a positive/negative and negative/positive order. All experiments were conducted in the two response modes; EoS and SbS. The results were the same as in their debtors scenario; no significant order or response mode effects for consistent evidence, while order effects were present for mixed evidence in the SbS mode when two pieces of mixed evidence were used, and in both response modes when four pieces of mixed evidence were used.

Depending on the same evidence used by Tubbs et al. (1990) in their creditors scenario, Messier (1992) conducted an experiment involving an audit judgement concerning unrecorded creditors. Mixed evidence was presented to the subjects in a SbS mode. The results confirmed that order of evidence was significant. However, it had no impact on the extent of audit testing.

The need to write down inventory is an evaluation-type task used in a study by Krull et al. (1993). Subjects of the study were asked to evaluate four pieces of mixed evidence relating to the valuation of the inventory and presented in a SbS mode. The study also included fraudulent signals as a variable to test its effect on auditors' beliefs. One group of the subjects was faced with fraud signals, while the other group completed the task with no such signals. The findings of the study suggest that the presence of fraudulent signals will affect the final opinion as it increased the final likelihood of insisting on an inventory write down. The results also indicated that experience affected auditors' judgements. Recency effects were more significant for experienced than for inexperienced auditors. This latter result contradicts with the findings of Messier and Tubbs (1994) that less experienced auditors showed significantly greater recency than more experienced auditors. Krull et al. (1993) claimed that this contradiction might be due to the difference between the two studies and to the difference in the experience levels examined in each study. Messier and Tubbs (1994) examined the difference in judgements between seniors and managers, while the subjects of Krull et al. (1993) were managers and senior managers.

A different evaluation-type task is that related to performance auditing. A study by Pei et al. (1992) included two scenarios involving an efficiency audit and an effectiveness audit. The subjects were asked to evaluate whether one particular state programme was managing and utilising its resources efficiently, and whether the desired results and benefits were effectively being achieved. Subjects were presented with four pieces of mixed evidence in a SbS mode. The results confirmed the predictions of the belief-adjustment model about the presence of recency effects. However, the order effect was not significant in the case of the efficiency audit.

The going concern judgement is an evaluation-type task addressed by Messier (1992). Subjects of his study were presented with four pieces of mixed evidence in a SbS mode. The results supported the presence of recency effects. However, these recency effects did not result in different levels of audit testing or in issuing different audit reports. Asare (1992) also employed a going concern evaluation task in testing for order effects. As with Messier (1992), Asare's study was based on the case of mixed evidence presented in a SbS mode. Furthermore, Asare (1992) used two belief frames; failure and viability. The results of his study indicated recency effects in all cases. Thus, the belief frame did not affect the existence of recency effects. Asare also arrived at a significant conclusion that recency effects affected auditors' reports. The results of the study indicated that auditors who evaluated evidence in a negative/positive order issued more unqualified opinions than those who evaluated evidence in a positive/negative order. This result contradicts with the findings of Messier (1992) that recency effects did not result in the issue of different audit reports.

The contradiction in the findings between Asare (1992) and Messier (1992) needs to be further investigated to corroborate one of the findings because of the important implication that this issue might have on the audit practice. The findings of Asare (1992) that recency affected auditors' decisions are more consistent with the predictions of the belief-adjustment model. Going back to the numerical example given earlier in this chapter, it is obvious that a belief of 84% strength would result in a different opinion than a belief of 28% strength. However, Kennedy (1993, p. 232) argues that the implications of Asare's findings 'would be less onerous for the profession if the audit review process mitigates recency'. Kennedy claims that accountability mitigates recency in auditors' judgements. Accountability refers to the requirement to justify one's judgement as a result of knowing that this judgement is going to be reviewed by auditors in a higher level.

Kennedy (1993) employed a going concern scenario to investigate the previous argument. Eight pieces of mixed evidence (four positive and four negative) were presented to the subjects in a SbS order. However, subjects were asked to make only one judgement after all pieces of evidenced were presented (EoS). Thus, the evaluation mode is an EoS rather than a SbS mode. Three accountability conditions were manipulated; no accountability, pre-accountability, and post-accountability.

Subjects in the no accountability group were told that their answers would be totally confidential and not traceable to anyone personally. Subjects in the pre-accountability group were told before evidence was presented to them that their responses would be reviewed, while subjects in the post-accountability group were told the same but after being presented with all pieces of evidence and before giving their final judgement. Subjects of the experiment were MBA students and audit managers.

The results of Kennedy's (1993) study indicated that recency effects were present in the responses of subjects in the no accountability and post-accountability group. However, judgements of subjects in the pre-accountability group exhibited no recency. This result supports the argument that accountability mitigates recency. This result is significant and could have serious practical implications on the audit profession. An important implication is that absence of accountability might lead to a change in the auditor's judgement which in turn affects the audit effectiveness. The results of Kennedy (1993) also indicated that experience mitigated recency which is consistent with Messier and Tubbs (1994) and Trotman and Wright (1996).

Cushing and Ahlawat (1996) argued that auditors are not likely to bias their judgements in real audit settings in response to the order in which they receive and evaluate pieces of evidence. They employed the same going concern scenario used by Asare (1992). However, they examined the effect of documentation on recency. Cushing and Ahlawat (1996) differentiated between accountability as referred to in Kennedy (1993) and documentation. Documentation involved asking the subjects of the experiment to write a memorandum to the senior partner providing reasons that would support their audit opinion. Furthermore, subjects were instructed to seal their experimental materials in an envelope and were guaranteed complete anonymity which means the absence of accountability. Cushing and Ahlawat (1996) conducted their experiment in a SbS mode with four pieces of mixed evidence. The results of their study supported the presence of recency effects. However, these effects were not present with the subjects who performed the documentation task. This means that documentation or providing a justification of an opinion mitigated recency effects.

Trotman and Wright (1996) also employed the same going concern scenario used by Asare (1992). They aimed at testing the effect of experience on recency. Subjects of their experiment were audit managers, seniors, and students. Four pieces of mixed evidence were used and both evidence evaluation modes were employed. Trotman and Wright considered the going concern task to be a complex task for both seniors and students and a simple one for managers. The results of their experiment indicated the presence of recency effects only for students and seniors. This means that experience mitigated recency effects which is consistent with their findings in the evaluation of internal controls task and the findings of Messier and Tubbs (1994). However, it contradicts the findings of Krull et al. (1993) that experience resulted in greater recency effects.

Estimation-type tasks have not received the same attention from auditing researchers as evaluation-type tasks. Kerr and Ward (1994) employed a scenario involving an estimation-type audit task which is planning the extent of testing a hypothetical client's debtors. The results of their study indicate that estimation tasks will result in judgements that fit averaging integration models and that experience has no effect on the integration rule employed.

Conclusions

This chapter presented a review of the auditing literature concerning the process of belief revision using the belief-adjustment model and its earlier version, the contrast/surprise model.

Previous audit studies that examined the validity of the predictions of both versions of the model supported the prediction of recency effects for short series of mixed evidence in the case of evaluation-type tasks. However, there is a lack of research to validate the order effect predictions in estimation-type tasks. The lack of research for long series of evidence is also obvious. This could be due to the difficulty of carrying out the experiments depending on long series of evidence as this would be time consuming.

Although validating the predictions of the belief-adjustment model, and its earlier version, the contrast/surprise model, was the focus of previous auditing studies, investigating the implications of the model's predictions has not received much attention. The implications of the model's predictions could be significant to the audit process. The findings of Asare (1992) that recency resulted in different audit judgements have important implications on the effectiveness of the audit process. However, this finding was not supported by Messier (1992) who found that recency effects did not result in different levels of audit testing or in different audit reports.

Furthermore, the contradiction between the findings of Kennedy (1993), Messier and Tubbs (1994), and Trotman and Wright (1996) and the findings of Krull et al. (1993) about the relationship between experience and recency leads to another important implication. Where experience mitigates or increases recency, this means that auditors' judgements and evaluation of evidence are subject to change according to the level of the auditor.

The findings of Kennedy (1993) and Cushing and Ahlawat (1996) that accountability and documentation mitigated recency also point out to an important issue. This issue is concerned with the possibility of the change in auditors' decisions due to accountability and documentation, which might have important implications on the audit practice.

In addition to the importance of considering the previous implications, there are other issues that the previous auditing studies did not address. These issues include the following:
- Do auditors follow a belief revision behaviour or approach in practice?
- Does the difference in the response or evaluation mode lead to different audit opinions?
- How does the belief revision approach affect the efficiency and effectiveness of the audit process?

Chapter 3

Factors Affecting Auditors' Belief Revisions

Introduction

The belief revision approach, as has been indicated, involves forming an initial belief and then updating or revising this belief according to new pieces of confirming and disconfirming evidence. Auditors' formation of the initial belief and the weight assigned by them to pieces of evidence will depend on a number of factors. These factors have not actually been agreed upon, and no specific list of them has been suggested. However, a review of the auditing literature, indicates that factors affecting auditors' formation of the initial belief and their attitudes toward confirming and disconfirming evidence can be classified into seven factors. These factors are belief formation, confirmation bias, diagnostic content of evidence, expertise, professional scepticism, motivational factors, and cognitive factors. The aim of this chapter is to discuss the main findings of previous auditing studies concerning the effect of these factors.

The following points are addressed in this chapter:
- Belief formation.
- Confirmation bias.
- Diagnostic content of evidence.
- Expertise.
- Professional scepticism.
- Motivational factors.
- Cognitive factors.

Belief Formation

Research in audit decision-making has emphasised the importance of belief formation because of its effect on information search and evaluation (Libby, 1985; Bedard and Biggs, 1991; and Einhorn, 1976). As auditing is an ill-structured task, it requires the auditor to form and revise beliefs to help structure the task (Einhorn, 1976). Beliefs help auditors focus information search and evaluation, thus making the auditing process more tractable (Peters, 1990). The importance of belief formation is also demonstrated by the American professional standards for analytical procedures that call for auditors to hypothesise likely causes of unexpected patterns in financial statement balances and to develop plans to investigate (AICPA, 1988, SAS 56). Therefore, audit efficiency and effectiveness depend on competency in recognising patterns in financial data and in hypothesising likely causes of these patterns to serve as a guide for further testing (Bedard and Biggs, 1991). Although some studies suggested the importance of belief formation to auditors, this suggestion has not received empirical support. Rather, previous studies were concerned mainly with the effect of the initial belief on auditors' attitudes toward confirming and disconfirming evidence.

The effect of auditors' beliefs on their evaluation of evidence can be either due to the source of these beliefs or due to their frame.

Source of Belief

Two sources of beliefs have been identified; generated beliefs and inherited beliefs (Church, 1990). Generated beliefs refer to beliefs formulated by the auditor himself/herself. An inherited belief, on the other hand, refers to beliefs provided to the auditor. Church (1990) and Church and Schneider (1993) suggested that auditors might inherit their beliefs from various sources. Inherited beliefs could be:
- suggested by the auditor's superiors,
- obtained from decision aids such as expert systems or decision support systems,
- suggested by client personnel, or
- obtained from pervious years' working papers.

Self-generated beliefs depend on creativity or what is called the critical imagination and the ability to vary the range over which beliefs are generated (Popper, 1977) and is retrieved from long term memory (Church and Schneider, 1993). Eltsein et al. (1978) confirm the need for this ability to generate a diverse set of beliefs. This ability consistently leads to a correct diagnosis being made.

Ismail and Trotman (1995) examined the effect of the review process on the generation of beliefs in an analytical review task. The review process refers to the review of the work done by an auditor by another member of the audit team of equal or higher rank. The results of the study indicated that the review process resulted in more plausible beliefs being generated by the reviewer especially when the review process involved discussion between the reviewer and the reviewee.

In a study by Kida (1984), he reported that a number of psychological studies concluded that the source of belief had no effect on evidence search. The overwhelming conclusion was that individuals preferentially collected evidence that tended to confirm, rather than disconfirm, their beliefs regardless of the source of these beliefs. In addition, it appeared not to matter where the inherited belief originated, how likely it was that the belief would prove accurate or inaccurate, or whether substantial incentives for accurate belief revision were offered.

However, Kida's conclusions were not supported in audit settings. Previous auditing studies concluded that the source of belief could affect auditors' commitment to their beliefs, and thus affects their search for evidence. In other words, auditors who feel committed to their beliefs will try to confirm them. This commitment will depend to a great extent on the source of the belief. A few studies in the auditing literature have addressed this issue.

Bedard and Biggs (1991) conducted a laboratory study in which 21 auditors were asked to think aloud while performing an analytical procedures task. One of the results of their study indicated that a number of subjects had difficulty in evaluating or updating beliefs. One of the auditors who at one point proposed the correct belief, was unable to disconfirm an early belief. This auditor and seven others did not disconfirm their self-generated beliefs, even though disconfirming pieces of evidence had already been acquired. This result indicates that auditors are fully committed to generated beliefs to the extent that they are not able to disconfirm them, even if these generated beliefs were wrong. However, this result cannot be generalised because there are some limitations on Bedard and Biggs' study. First, their study contains less information than the real audit environment. Second, consultation with other members of the audit team was not available, which does not acknowledge the reality of the situation. Third, they conducted their study using verbal protocol procedures that may not provide a complete trace of all thoughts during a decision process.

Some studies also addressed the implications of the different sources of inherited beliefs on auditors' attitudes toward confirming and disconfirming evidence. In a study by Chung and Monroe (1996), a going concern evaluation task was employed to test the effect of beliefs suggested by auditors' superiors on their decisions. Subjects of their study were auditing students. Chung and Monroe (1996) concluded that students who inherited beliefs from an instructor rated confirming evidence more important than disconfirming evidence, while those who generated their own beliefs did not. Although this study provides some guidance about the effect of beliefs inherited from instructors (or superiors), the results are limited because the subjects of the study were students and not practising auditors.

Church and Schneider (1993) also investigated the effect a superior's suggestion on auditors' generation of additional beliefs. They concluded that auditors who inherited a superior's suggestion from a particular transaction cycle generated fewer additional beliefs from the same transaction cycle than did auditors who were not provided with a superior's suggestion. An example of the previous conclusion is that 'if there is an unexpected fluctuation in a client's gross margin ratio. The cause is believed to be a problem with either the sales or purchases transaction cycle. If the auditor's superior suggests a specific sales problem which is sales cut-off error as being the cause. The likelihood of retrieving additional sales problems is affected whereas the likelihood of retrieving purchases problems is likely to be unaffected' (Church and Schneider, 1993, pp. 336-337).

The results of Church and Schneider (1993) indicate that auditors are committed to beliefs suggested by their superiors which is consistent with the findings of Chung and Monroe (1996). An important consequence of this finding is that auditors might try to confirm beliefs suggested by their superiors even if these beliefs were not correct.

Kaplan et al. (1992) suggest that the use of decision aids in the audit process provides the auditor with beliefs that could plausibly explain ratio fluctuations discovered in an analytical review. The trend for firms to adopt such decision aids overcomes potential difficulties auditors might have in retrieving beliefs from memory. However, the problem with decision aids is that the auditors will still have to assess the plausibility of the beliefs provided by these aids. Although Kaplan's suggestion about the benefits of employing decision aids in generating beliefs might hold true, the main consideration here is whether these decision aids are practically used by accounting firms. This consideration together with the lack of studies on the effect of such source of inherited beliefs on auditors' attitudes toward evidence, might not provide a clear insight about the effect of using decision aids on the belief revision process.

Another source of inherited beliefs is the client's personnel. Taking into consideration the conservative and sceptical nature of the auditors and their training, one might arrive at a conclusion that auditors would tend to disconfirm beliefs suggested by the clients' personnel. However, the findings of previous studies did not support this view. Anderson and Koonce (1995) found that some factors affect auditors acceptance of client suggested beliefs. They concluded that when auditors conduct analytical procedures, client suggested cause of fluctuation was accepted when auditors found evidence indicating that this suggested cause accounted substantially for all of the fluctuation. However, when the client suggested cause was insufficient to explain the fluctuation, auditors' acceptance of this cause varied. Auditors who quantified the implications of the cause realised its insufficiency, while those who failed to quantify did not.

Koonce and Phillips (1996) also examined the effect of client suggested causes of fluctuations on auditors' decisions. They found that when a client suggested a non-error cause, auditors judged the cause to be more plausible when the information pertaining to that cause was easy to comprehend. In other words, when auditors were able to identify and integrate relevant pieces of information that enabled them to evaluate whether the client suggested cause fully accounted for the observed fluctuation, they were more willing to accept the cause. This finding supports the findings of Anderson and Koonce (1995).

The implication that different sources of beliefs might result in different attitudes toward confirming and disconfirming evidence might have significant consequences on the effectiveness of the audit process. Effectiveness might be affected if the weight assigned to a certain piece of evidence differed depending upon the source of the auditor's beliefs. This might lead to different audit opinions which, in its turn, would affect the effectiveness of the audit process.

Belief Frame

According to the belief frame, auditors' beliefs concerning the fairness of a client's financial statements can take one of two broad frames:
1. That a material error exists in the financial statements, and this is called the error frame.

2. That no material error exists and any changes in the financial statements are attributed to environmental factors, and this is called the environmental frame.

The effect of the belief frame on auditors' search for evidence has been investigated by a few auditing studies. McMillan and White (1993) concluded that auditors who favoured the error frame acted in a confirmatory manner, while auditors who favoured the environmental frame acted in a disconfirmatory manner due to professional scepticism. Their findings seem to be true when the effect of the belief frame is isolated from other factors. However, this might not be the case if the belief frame is combined with other factors especially auditors' commitment to their beliefs. The findings of previous studies that auditors are committed to their self-generated beliefs contradicts with the findings of McMillan and White that auditors who favoured the environmental frame acted in a disconfirmatory manner.

Heiman-Hoffman et al. (1995) found that difference in the error frame itself could affect auditors' performance. They concluded that auditors who generated a very frequent error as their initial belief performed best when it was the actual error, but performed worst when it was not. However, auditors who generated a less frequent error as their initial belief performed moderately well in all cases. The reason for this was that auditors who chose the very frequent error as their initial belief found it difficult to switch beliefs.

If confirmatory strategies are employed by auditors, the final decisions will depend on the initial framing of the belief (Kida, 1984). Kida added that to overcome search biases, the decision task could be presented so as to force consideration of alternative beliefs. For example, a simple listing of data relevant for testing competing beliefs may be employed, or the beliefs to be tested could initially be framed to avoid making the most costly error. Kida (1984) conducted a study, in which 77 partners and managers participated, to test whether auditors attend to more confirmatory evidence, disconfirmatory evidence, or equal amounts of both when testing a belief. Auditors were given alternative beliefs depending on their experimental group. Results indicated that the belief framing had some impact on the type of information auditors searched for, providing limited support for confirmatory strategies. However, this result cannot be generalised because subjects of the study were provided with the beliefs to be tested, thus excluding the effect of the source of beliefs.

Although the studies concerning the effect of the source of beliefs and belief frame on auditors' attitudes toward confirming and disconfirming evidence are important to the understanding of the way auditors assign weight to different pieces of evidence, these studies did not address an important issue about the formation of initial beliefs. This issue is related to whether auditors form initial beliefs or not. Of great importance also is knowing the sort of initial beliefs that auditors might form. Most of the previous studies concentrated on beliefs in the form of plausible causes for unexpected fluctuations in the financial statements, or initial likelihood assessments whether these assessments were related to the evaluation of the internal controls or a certain account balance or whether they were related to a going concern decision. However, from a practical point of view, there is an obvious lack of auditing studies concerning the meaning of the initial belief for auditors and the extent to which auditors form initial beliefs in practice. Addressing these issues might help in providing a better understanding of auditors' approaches in searching for and evaluating evidence.

Confirmation Bias

Prior research in psychology showed that people are usually confirmatory biased (see for example Mynatt et al., 1978; Darley and Gross, 1983; Klayman and Ha, 1987; and Davidsson and Wahlund, 1992). Stated differently, people usually seek information which is consistent with their beliefs. However, research in auditing found just the opposite. In a study by Butt and Campbell (1989), the results suggested that unless specifically requested to do so, auditors do not generally seek confirming evidence.

Research by Ashton and Ashton (1988) and Tubbs et al. (1990) also suggest that auditors will readily revise their beliefs in response to new evidence and that they are particularly sensitive to disconfirming evidence.

Ashton and Ashton's (1990) study supported the previous results that auditors are more sensitive to disconfirming evidence. They conducted four experiments in two auditing and two non-auditing tasks and concluded that the auditors were more responsive to disconfirming evidence than to confirming evidence. They also conducted two additional experiments, in the same non-auditing tasks, which showed that another group of professional subjects (business executives) are confirmatory biased.

The same result that auditors are not confirmatory biased was supported by Boritz (1998). Subjects of the study were experienced auditors and students. The results indicated that the auditors were not subject to the same confirmation bias as students. Thus, concluding that auditors do not display the confirmation bias observed in the psychological literature.

The result that auditors are more sensitive to disconfirming evidence might not be surprising. Although people in general might seek to confirm their beliefs, auditors, on the other hand, might tend to do the opposite. The training of the auditors together with their responsibility toward third parties and the nature of the audit process might all be factors forcing auditors to assign more weight to disconfirming evidence. However, a study by Ayers and Kaplan (1993) concluded that auditors are prone to use confirming strategies when making information choices in an analytical procedure task. Another study by Chung and Monroe (1996) also concluded that in some cases auditors demonstrated a belief confirming strategy. Their findings indicated that auditors who were asked to provide an explanation for their judgement, were more prone to confirming evidence, while those who were asked for a counter-explanation were not.

Bamber et al. (1997) also found that auditors are confirmatory biased in that they are more sensitive to evidence that confirms their initial beliefs even with the difference in their experience levels.

Tan (1995) examined the effect of prior audit involvement on evidence search strategies. The findings of the study indicated that auditors with prior audit involvement were more sensitive to evidence confirming their beliefs compared to those who took over the current year's audit from another auditor.

The findings that auditors are more sensitive, in some cases, to confirming evidence imply the need for further research about auditors' attitudes toward confirming and disconfirming evidence. However, an important issue here is whether auditors in practice assign weight to evidence depending on whether it is confirming or disconfirming. On the theoretical level, it has always been assumed that auditors assign weight to evidence depending on its source. Third party written evidence is assigned more weight than internal dependent evidence. The relationship between the source of evidence and whether it is confirming or disconfirming on one hand and the weight assigned to evidence on the other hand lacks its empirical support.

Diagnostic Content of Evidence

The diagnostic content of evidence might be an important factor that affects auditors' search for evidence. However, previous auditing studies have not directly addressed the effect of the diagnostic content on auditors' search for evidence. In addition to this, the problem with the diagnostic content of evidence is not only how auditors react toward diagnostic and non-diagnostic evidence, but the problem is related also to what is meant by the term 'diagnostic content of evidence'. The following discussion might help in understanding the meaning of 'diagnostic evidence' and auditors' attitudes toward this type of evidence.

Hackenbrack (1992) investigated the role that non-diagnostic evidence, which he considers a priori irrelevant, can have on audit judgement. He conducted a laboratory experiment in which audit seniors assessed how much company's exposure to fraudulent reporting changed during a year, given a mixture of diagnostic and non-diagnostic evidence. He considered three types of non-diagnostic evidence: favourable and unfavourable (collectively called non-neutral) and neutral. In a fraud-risk setting or an error frame, favourable non-diagnostic evidence describes client's features an auditor would find encouraging, such as the client's willingness to prepare schedules requested by the auditor. Unfavourable non-diagnostic evidence describes negative client's features, such as the recording of a recurring transaction effectively but not efficiently. Neutral non-diagnostic evidence includes routine, unexceptional items like the organisational chart. The findings of Hackenbrack suggest that auditors, given a mix of diagnostic and non-diagnostic evidence, made decisions that were less extreme (more regressive) than those made using only diagnostic evidence. He stated that the magnitude of the observed effect was in some cases directly related to the capacity of the non-diagnostic evidence to hold the auditor's attention.

The effect of non-diagnostic evidence in making less extreme decisions is known as the dilution effect (Nisbett et al., 1981). Glover (1997) extended the work of Hackenbrack (1992) to investigate whether auditors exhibit the dilution effect when faced with time pressure and accountability. He concluded that time pressure reduced, but did not eliminate, the dilution effect. However, accountability had no significant effect.

In the study by Ayers and Kaplan (1993), their main finding was that auditors are prone to use confirming strategies when making information choices in an analytical procedure task. This finding contradicts with findings of other auditing studies which proved that auditors are disconfirming biased. Ayers and Kaplan attributed their finding to that auditors might merely have believed that the confirming pieces of evidence were more diagnostic.

It is not very clear from the previous studies what is considered to be diagnostic audit evidence and what is considered to be non-diagnostic. While Hackenbrack (1992) referred to diagnostic evidence as relevant evidence and non-diagnostic evidence as irrelevant evidence, Ayers and Kaplan's (1993) study does not imply the same. If irrelevant evidence is considered as non-diagnostic, then the results of Hackenbrack's study might have significant implications on the efficiency of the audit process. Hackenbrack's study concluded that auditors' decisions would be less extreme if they were presented with diagnostic and non-diagnostic evidence. This would simply mean that in order to arrive at less extreme or moderate results auditors have to gather both diagnostic (relevant) and non-diagnostic (irrelevant) evidence, which in its turn means more time spent and more costs incurred, and hence a less efficient audit.

Studies in the area of information gathering in general do not provide a clear insight into the meaning of diagnosticity, even though some studies that investigated the effect of confirmatory and diagnosing strategies in social information gathering showed that diagnosticity is the major determinant of the information-gathering preferences (Trope and Bassok, 1982). Skov and Sherman (1986) pointed out that research in information-gathering strategies suggests that people can employ one of three strategies of information seeking.

The first strategy of information seeking is a confirmatory one under which evidence is being sought to the extent that it is more likely under the belief being tested than under the alternative. The second strategy is also a confirmatory strategy under which people will tend to gather information that will have the effect of making the belief under test appear to be true. The third strategy is a diagnosing strategy under which people prefer evidence that is most differentially probable under the belief and the alternative. The findings of Skov and Sherman supported the predominance of the diagnosing strategy and a less significant tendency to follow the confirming strategies.

McMillan and White (1993) indicated that diagnostic evidence is evidence that allows auditors to distinguish between alternative beliefs, which contradicts with Skov and Sherman (1986). In addition, the definitions of McMillan and White (1993) and Skov and Sherman (1986) of diagnostic evidence in relation to the belief under consideration are different from the definition of Hackenbrack (1992) of diagnostic evidence as relevant evidence and non-diagnostic evidence as irrelevant evidence.

Troutman and Shanteau (1977, p. 43) gave the following example of non-diagnostic evidence:

> Suppose you have planned an experiment that you are fairly certain will confirm a particular hypothesis. Then you read two relevant studies by equally well-respected colleagues and one study supports your hypothesis while the other disconfirms it. ... If the two studies are equally well done, they cancel each other out so that the total value of the information is nondiagnostic.

Although the previous example does not give a clear definition of non-diagnostic evidence, it indicates that evidence is diagnostic when it enables the confirmation (or disconfirmation) of a certain belief, which supports the views of McMillan and White (1993). Perhaps a better illustration of the meaning of diagnostic evidence is that provided by Wallendael and Guignard (1992, pp. 25-26) as follows:

> For example, a physician using a confirmation strategy may make an initial assumption about the most likely cause of a patient's malaise, assume that disease Q is probably responsible, and then check for symptoms that are consistent with that particular diagnosis. This approach may lead to reliance on rather nondiagnostic information; for instance, a diagnosis may be based on the presence of symptoms A, B, and C, which are also common to disease Z. A physician using a diagnosing strategy, by contrast, would attempt to distinguish between diseases Q and Z by questioning his or her patient about symptom D, which is almost always present in Z but rarely in Q.

This means that diagnostic evidence, as compared to non-diagnostic evidence, is evidence that distinguishes between the belief under consideration and its alternatives, thus allowing the confirmation or disconfirmation of the belief. This definition is consistent with Troutman and Shanteau (1977) and McMillan and White (1993). However, it is not consistent with Hackenbrack (1992) in that non-diagnostic evidence is irrelevant evidence. Rather, non-diagnostic evidence is evidence that could not be used on its own to confirm or disconfirm a belief.

Expertise

Auditors' expertise has been focus of many auditing studies not only those related to belief revision. However, the concept of expertise is still debatable. While expertise can be defined (Bedard, 1989) as the possession of a large body of knowledge and procedural skill, it has been argued (Davis and Solomon, 1989) that a performance-based notion of expertise is most appropriate. Expertise has also been defined in association with performance in a particular task domain (Frensch and Sternberg, 1989; and Bonner and Lewis, 1990).

The role of professional expertise in auditing decisions is significant for a number of reasons. Many judgements made by the auditor are subjective. Also, the cognitive psychology literature suggests that the quality of decisions improves with experience (Colbert, 1989). Auditors with different amounts of professional experience or with specialised experience in various industries might have different audit strategies (Krogstad et al., 1984). However, the use of these different audit strategies by professionals with various levels of experience is not, in and of itself, cause for concern since different approaches can lead different auditors to similar conclusions. But problems might arise if differing strategies lead some auditors to either under-audit (of primary concern because audit risk may rise above acceptable levels) or over-audit (of secondary concern because the audit is presumably effective although it may be inefficient) (Colbert, 1989).

Although expertise is a very important factor in the area of belief revision because it would have an effect on auditors' initial beliefs and the weight they assign to different pieces of evidence, only a few studies examined its effect in this area. In fact our knowledge about expertise in auditing in general is very limited (Bedard and Michelene, 1993).

Bedard and Biggs (1991) investigated the effect of expertise on belief formation. They conducted a laboratory study in which 21 auditors were asked to think aloud while performing an analytical procedures task. One of their results indicated that belief formation was the stage at which process errors most frequently occurred, and the least experienced auditors had the most difficulty at that stage. Among the problems the least experienced auditors faced in generating the plausible belief (the belief which is supported by evidence), were addressing only part of a recognised pattern, and fixating on a certain error type.

Biggs and Mock (1983) compared the audit scope decisions relating to debtors confirmation of two inexperienced and two experienced audit seniors. Each auditor was required to think aloud while making sample-size decisions. They concluded that experienced auditors tended to approach the problem by relying on stored information from prior experience, which was brought to bear on developing an overall picture of the firm. The less experienced auditors tended to handle the problem in an ad hoc serial processing fashion because it appears that they were unable to organise the wide range of information that was given. They were forced to divide the information into smaller portions.

Experts might also rely more heavily on rules of thumb and examine more years of data than the novices. Bouwman (1984) found that experts tend to develop a 'feeling'or 'picture'of the firm. Experts did this by summarising groups of related findings, forming beliefs, and using a list of typical problems. Novices employed a passive, sequential strategy to examine the information.

Wright and Wright (1997) addressed the impact of industry experience on forming beliefs of likely errors in conducting analytical procedures. Their findings indicated that industry experience enhanced the formation of beliefs in identifying errors but did not affect risk assessments or revisions to planned extent.

It could not, however, be concluded that just because an auditor has many years of experience s/he would generate a plausible belief in every situation, or even in a majority of the situations encountered. In addition, expertise might also have some unwanted effects. Experienced auditors seldom receive outcome feedback, and so bad habits may go uncorrected (Davis and Solomon, 1989). This might be due to the experienced auditors' overconfidence of themselves, and thus they might fall into the trap of generating and testing implausible beliefs.

The results of the previous studies that experienced auditors tend to develop their initial beliefs much more easier than inexperienced auditors do not seem surprising. It is expected that with more experience, one can have better understanding and more ability to form beliefs especially self-generated ones. Moreover, the findings that less experienced auditors might have difficulty in forming their initial beliefs might not affect the audit practice. Practically, most of the audit work is done as a team, and in this case auditors would share their experiences to be able to form their beliefs. It is also worth noting that, as indicated by previous studies, the initial beliefs would be formed at the stage of the audit planning and preparing the audit strategy. In this case the formation of the initial beliefs would be the duty of experienced auditors.

The relationship between expertise and evidence search strategies has also been investigated. Kaplan and Reckers (1989) conducted a study where auditors were given the results of analytical tests and asked to assess the likelihood that observed abnormalities were due to accounting error or irregularity as distinct from environmental change. They were also asked to indicate the information they would seek in response to the test results. The results indicated that for relatively inexperienced auditors, their initial beliefs will positively correlate with the type of information they will subsequently seek. In other words, inexperienced auditors will follow a confirming search strategy. For relatively experienced auditors, the results showed that their initial beliefs will not correlate with the type of information sought but rather they will follow a balanced information search strategy. These findings provide evidence that audit experience acts to moderate the information seeking judgements of auditors and that more experience is associated with more conservative information-seeking judgements. These results were reached using a rank measure of information seeking. However, a second measure of information seeking based on unranked questions did not support these results.

McMillan and White (1996) extended the work of Kaplan and Reckers (1989) by studying a much wider range of audit experience and creating a wider range of initial material error assessments. They concluded that only staff auditors exhibited confirmatory evidence search strategies while more experienced auditors exhibited a balanced search strategy. This result is consistent with the result of Kaplan and Reckers (1989) when they depended on a rank measure of information seeking. McMillan and White (1996) also concluded that experienced auditors had higher material error assessments than inexperienced auditors. This latter result contradicts with the findings of Anderson and Maletta (1994) who found that inexperienced auditors were more sensitive to evidence indicating unfavourable characteristics of a client. This was further reflected in control risk assessments in that auditing students rated control risk to be higher than audit seniors.

The findings that experience will help in moderating or balancing the evidence search strategy support the results of Messier and Tubbs (1994) and Trotman and

Wright (1996) presented in chapter 2 that experience helps in mitigating recency effects. Undoubtedly, experience in most cases would improve the effectiveness and efficiency of the audit process. However, it is reasonable to assume that the audit process is conducted with inexperienced as well as experienced auditors in the team.

Professional Scepticism

Professional scepticism could be defined as 'a choice to fulfil the professional auditor's duty to prevent or reduce the harmful consequences of another person's behavior. Specifically, this means being willing to doubt, question or disagree with client assertions or generally accepted conclusions' (Shaub and Lawrence, 1996, p. 126).

Although auditors are probably thought to be sceptical because of their training and their liability to third parties, the effect of professional scepticism on auditors' initial beliefs and their search for and evaluation of evidence has not received much attention. The study conducted by McMillan and White (1993) pointed out that many auditors might consider error-bias behaviour favourable because it indicates a responsiveness to professional scepticism and a demonstration of conservatism. However, they suggested that the actual strength and role of this decision bias needs further investigation because of its potential effects on the efficiency and effectiveness of audit decision-making.

The results of McMillan and White (1993) imply that professional scepticism would affect both the initial belief frame and auditors' attitudes toward confirming and disconfirming evidence. If auditors put their initial beliefs in an error-frame, they would tend to confirm these beliefs (McMillan and White, 1993). The risk here arises when the initial error-framed beliefs are implausible. The result would be a decrease in either the effectiveness or the efficiency of the audit. Effectiveness might be affected if auditors tended to confirm their initial implausible beliefs. Efficiency, on the other hand, would be affected if evidence confirming the initial belief was not found, and thus, auditors would have to re-plan their work. In addition to that, an approach that is too conservative might lead to the performance of unnecessary audit procedures and thereby reduces audit efficiency.

The findings of Knechel and Messier (1990) indicated that negative evidence, in general, led to greater judgement revisions by auditors than positive evidence, and the most reliable negative evidence led to the greatest revisions. This finding is a demonstration of the sceptical behaviour of auditors. However, Knechel and Messier stated two limitations to their study. First, it was assumed that auditors evaluate each piece of evidence sequentially, which might not be true. Second, because the evidence provided to the subjects was of a subjective nature, not all auditors might have perceived it to be positive or negative.

The findings of a study by Krishnamoorthy et al. (1997) illustrated the relationship between professional scepticism and the formation of beliefs. They concluded that the conservative and sceptical nature of auditors led them to generate more beliefs when financial and non-financial information signalled a decline than when the information signalled a stable environment. In addition, more beliefs were formed when the decline was signalled by financial rather than non-financial information.

Motivational Factors

The effect of motivational factors on auditors' search for and evaluation of evidence has not received much attention from auditing researchers. Church (1990) suggested that there are two sets of motivational factors that might have an effect on auditors' strategies in searching for evidence. These two sets are cognitive consistency and seeking the approval of others. Cognitive consistency refers to maintaining a consistent set of cognitions. Inconsistent cognitions will arise from disconfirming evidence, and this is why auditors who are strongly committed to their beliefs might ignore disconfirming evidence. Auditors might also be motivated to seek the approval of others specially their superiors and their clients (Staw and Ross, 1987; and Simon and Francis, 1988). This could lead auditors to follow a confirmatory strategy when searching for evidence even if their beliefs were implausible. This is what led Church (1990) to suggest the importance of investigating the effect of this motivational factor on auditors' search for evidence.

Motivational factors are, therefore, expressed in terms of auditors' commitment to their initial beliefs which, in turn, might affect the effectiveness and efficiency of the audit process. Effectiveness might be affected if auditors have motivations to confirm their beliefs even if these beliefs are implausible. Efficiency, on the other hand, would be affected if auditors were motivated to search for evidence confirming implausible beliefs. If this evidence did not exist, the auditors might consequently change their beliefs and start another search for evidence confirming their new beliefs. This would obviously mean more time and cost and, hence, a less efficient audit. Thus, the implications of motivational factors on the effectiveness and efficiency of the audit process might be significant.

Church (1991) investigated the effect of motivational factors on auditors' decisions. Motivational factors were reflected by manipulating auditors' commitment to their initial beliefs. Commitment was manipulated by asking subjects in the strongly committed group to provide written justifications of their initial beliefs, and were told that their justifications would be discussed with representatives from their firms. Subjects' names and affiliations also appeared at the top of the paper on which they wrote their justifications. The results indicated that auditors who were strongly committed to their beliefs evaluated evidence as being more consistent with their beliefs than auditors who were not strongly committed, and assigned more weight to confirming evidence. This means that the aim to maintain cognitive consistency and seek the approval of others might lead auditors to misinterpret disconfirming evidence or under-weigh it. The results of Church (1991) also indicated that auditors who were strongly committed to their beliefs had better recall of disconfirming evidence. Church explained that the reason behind this is that auditors who are strongly committed to their beliefs will be motivated to explain away any inconsistencies associated with disconfirming evidence. Thus, auditors would have better abilities of recalling disconfirming evidence because of the time and effort spent in evaluating this type of evidence.

Cognitive Factors

Cognitive factors are related mainly to belief formation and evidence explanations (Evans, 1987). Church (1990) suggests that there are three sets of cognitive factors; knowledge structures, recency and frequency, and remembering confirming and disconfirming evidence.

The organisation of auditors' knowledge structures in a way that enables more efficient use of memory capacity could result in a more effective auditing performance (Salthouse, 1991). Prior studies showed that experts in general are able to store knowledge in ways that allow them to perform tasks efficiently (Church, 1990). However, the organisation of auditors' knowledge structures is not well understood.

Auditors were found to rely on their judgements of the frequency of occurrence of financial statement errors when forming beliefs in an analytical review task (Libby, 1985). Church (1990) suggests that the likelihood that an item is accessed from the memory is directly affected by the recency and frequency with which it has been accessed previously. Auditors might be able to access explanations to errors that occur more frequently especially those that occurred recently. This could, in its turn, affect auditors' abilities to access alternative beliefs and explanations for evidence.

Auditors' memories have a significant effect on their decision-making (Johnson, 1994). Social research findings (Srull, 1981; and Hastie, 1980) demonstrated that individuals in general can remember disconfirming information better than confirming information. This conclusion is supported in audit settings by the findings of Church (1991) that auditors have better recall of disconfirming evidence. However, it is worth noting that the effect of auditors' memories of confirming and disconfirming evidence on their search and evaluation process would to a great extent be related to their documentation of gathered pieces of evidence. As auditors are expected to document all evidence gathered, then their memories of confirming and disconfirming evidence might not really affect the audit process.

Cognitive factors, especially knowledge structures and frequency of errors could not be separated from auditors' experience. Understanding the effect of these factors on auditors' search for evidence would be part of understanding the effect of experience. As experienced auditors are expected to have better knowledge structures and are more likely to have experience with more types of errors, they are expected to be more able to form their initial beliefs and provide plausible explanations for errors.

Conclusions

This chapter presented a review of the auditing literature on factors affecting auditors' belief revision. The factors reviewed in this chapter are belief formation, confirmation bias, diagnostic content of evidence, expertise, professional scepticism, and motivational and cognitive factors. These factors might affect auditors' initial beliefs of a client's financial statements and the weight they assign to different pieces of confirming and disconfirming evidence.

Although the results of previous auditing studies provide some indications about auditors' formation of initial beliefs and their attitudes toward confirming and disconfirming evidence, these studies were mainly concerned with the effects not the process itself. The previous studies were concerned with investigating the effect of different sources and frames of beliefs on auditors' preferences of confirming and disconfirming evidence. The issue of whether auditors in practice form initial beliefs or not has not been addressed. In addition to this, when studying the effect of the source of beliefs, it has been assumed that auditors would get their beliefs from one source at a time. Practically, this might not be true. If auditors were to form an initial belief, it would probably be a combination of their knowledge about the client and the business, the information they gather from the client personnel, and the suggestions of members of the audit team. Investigating the effect of a particular source in this case might not be possible.

The main finding of previous auditing studies is that auditors are more sensitive to disconfirming evidence (for example Knechel and Messier, 1990; Ashton and Ashton, 1988 and 1990; Tubbs et al., 1990; and Boritz, 1998). However, some exceptions to this were also found. Auditors who generated their beliefs and who inherited them from their superiors were more sensitive to confirming evidence (Bedard and Biggs, 1990; and Chung and Monroe, 1996). Auditors who favoured the error frame also acted in a confirmatory manner (McMillan and White, 1993). Justification of auditors' decisions was another factor that made auditors demonstrate a confirmatory search strategy (Church, 1991; and Chung and Monroe, 1996).

The previous findings about auditors' attitudes to evidence are probably based on the assumption that auditors will follow a belief revision approach and classify evidence to confirming and disconfirming. If auditors in practice do not adopt this classification of evidence, then the previous findings, although beneficial on a theoretical level, might not be of benefit on a practical level.

To conclude, although previous auditing studies arrived at results that provide better understanding of factors underlying auditors' strategies in their search for and evaluation of evidence, the results are still in need of further investigation and the following issues need to be addressed:

- Do auditors in practice form initial beliefs?
- How do auditors form their beliefs? Or in other words, what are practically the sources of auditors' beliefs?
- Do auditors differentiate between evidence depending on whether it is confirming or disconfirming?

Chapter 4

Empirical Research Design

Introduction

Chapters 2 and 3 represented a review of the belief revision approach in evidence search and evaluation including the belief-adjustment model and factors affecting auditors' formation of their initial beliefs and their attitudes toward confirming and disconfirming evidence. The review of the previous literature revealed the lack of studies addressing the relevance of employing the belief revision approach in audit settings. Most of the previous auditing studies were either concerned with validating the predictions of the belief-adjustment model or with investigating auditors' attitudes toward confirming and disconfirming evidence.

This chapter represents the design of the empirical study that aims mainly at exploring the auditing practice to find out about auditors' approaches in evaluating evidence, and comparing between these approaches and the belief revision approach.

The following points are addressed in this chapter:
- Aim of empirical study and research questions.
- Research methodology.

Aim of Empirical Study and Research Questions

The review of the previous auditing literature concerning the belief revision approach revealed that studies were either directed toward validating the predictions of the belief-adjustment model or toward investigating the effect of some factors, like belief source and frame, on auditors' attitudes toward confirming and disconfirming evidence. Importantly, there is a lack of auditing studies relating to the relevance of the belief revision approach to auditing. In other words, whether auditors follow a belief revision approach in practice. This issue points out to another related topic which is the benefits of employing a belief revision approach especially that there are several indications in the previous literature that employing a belief revision approach could affect the efficiency and effectiveness of the audit.

As well as the limitations of previous studies as identified above, there are other factors that still need to be practically investigated. These factors include the effect of the response mode on auditors' decisions, and the factors affecting the weight auditors assign to different pieces of evidence.

In particular, the empirical study is designed to address the following research questions:
1. Do auditors in practice follow a belief revision approach in their evaluation of evidence?
2. What are the factors that affect auditors' evaluation of evidence and, in particular factors affecting the formation of the initial beliefs and the weight assigned to different pieces of evidence?
3. Are there any benefits from following a belief revision approach in auditing particularly benefits related to improving the efficiency and effectiveness of the audit process?

Research Methodology

To achieve the aims of the study, a positivistic approach has been employed in which the collection of data depended on personal interviews and a laboratory experiment. The rationale for choosing these methods is discussed in this section.

The term methodology refers to the overall approach of the research process (Hussey and Hussey, 1997). In the social sciences, it is argued that there are two main approaches or paradigms from which research methodology can be derived: a positivistic, or quantitative, approach and a phenomenological, or qualitative, approach (Creswell, 1994; and Easterby-Smith et al., 1991).

The differentiation between the positivistic and phenomenological approaches is mainly based on the type of data collected and methods of analyses. The positivistic approach is concerned with collecting and analysing quantitative data in order to arrive at generalisable inferences which are often based on statistical analysis. The phenomenological approach, on the other hand, is concerned with collecting and analysing qualitative data in order to describe and/or explain a phenomenon in its context (Hussey and Hussey, 1997). In addition to this, in the positivistic approach, the researcher should be independent of what is being researched. In the phenomenological approach, on the other hand, the researcher interacts with what is being researched. This interaction can be in the form of living with or observing informants over a long period of time, or in the form of actual collaboration (Creswell, 1994).

Although the positivistic and phenomenological approaches are two extremes, it is unlikely that researchers, especially in social sciences, operate within their pure forms and the differences between the actual research methodologies adopted by the researchers are not clear cut (Hussey and Hussey, 1997).

The current research lends itself more to the positivistic approach. The empirical study depended on two methodologies; a survey research and an experimental study. The survey research depended on personal interviews with auditors to collect qualitative data about the audit practice concerning evidence evaluation strategies and issues related to factors affecting auditors' evaluation of evidence. Although the data collected here are qualitative, the way of analysing these data and the fact that the views of the researcher did not affect the interviewees make this more a positivistic rather than a phenomenological approach. In addition, the experimental study depended on the use of laboratory experiments to address the issue of comparing the belief revision approach to the actual approach followed by auditors in their search for and evaluation of evidence. The data have been analysed statistically, as discussed later. Thus, this methodology lends itself also to the positivistic approach. The two research methodologies, the survey research and experimental study are discussed in the following sections.

Survey Research

The lack of studies in the area of auditors' use of the belief revision approach in evidence evaluation highlights the need of exploring such an area before going further into investigating the benefits of the approach itself. The survey research is useful in this area as it provides with a convenient method for collecting data by asking people who have experienced certain phenomena to reconstruct these phenomena (Frankfort-Nachmias and Nachmias, 1992). Survey research includes mail questionnaires, personal interviews, and telephone interviews.

The current research employed the form of semi-structured personal interviews where an interview schedule has been prepared, however, the questions were left open-ended. This form of interviewing has been chosen for two reasons; first there was a list of issues about the audit practice that needed investigation. Second, the questions related to these issues could not be answered in the form of 'yes' or 'no' or any other pre-determined form. Rather, open-ended questions were more relevant to allow the interviewees to express their opinions freely. The interviews aimed at addressing the first two research questions which are:
1. Do auditors in practice follow a belief revision approach in their evaluation of evidence?
2. What are the factors that affect auditors' evaluation of evidence and, in particular factors affecting the formation of the initial beliefs and the weight assigned to different pieces of evidence?

The main drawback of depending on the interviews to find out about factors affecting auditors' evaluation of evidence is that previous studies depended on laboratory experiments which might limit the comparison of the results. However, conducting a laboratory experiment before carrying out the interviews was not possible because of the lack of information about the audit practice concerning the adoption of the belief revision approach.

The interview schedule[1] To answer the previous research questions, the interview schedule included questions related to the approach followed by auditors in their evaluation of evidence, and questions related to factors affecting this process. To find out about evidence evaluation approaches, two questions were included in the interview schedule. The first question was concerned with the steps of the audit process. The reason for asking this question was to find out whether the interviewees would mention anything about forming beliefs or following a belief revision approach without this being a leading question. The second question was a direct one about the formation of initial beliefs. This question has been included in the interview schedule in case the first question did not provide with a precise answer about the formation of initial beliefs.

The interview also included questions related to factors affecting auditors' evaluation of evidence. The factors discussed in the interview were those indicated in the previous literature about the belief revision approach and the belief-adjustment model. These factors included belief source and frame, expertise, confirmation bias, professional scepticism and conservatism, diagnostic content of evidence, and evidence order and evaluation mode. In addition, the interviewees were asked about the effect of time and cost on the evidence search process. The purpose of asking questions concerning these factors was to find out about their effects on auditors' evaluation of evidence with the aim to provide some insight into the audit practice and compare the findings with those from previous auditing studies.

Pilot testing It was beneficial to start with a pilot study of the interview schedule. Five members of the academic staff at the University of the West of England, who had previous experience in auditing, each agreed to participate in the pilot study.

One important issue that directed the interviews was whether auditors form beliefs at the beginning of the audit process. The interviewees agreed that auditors do not form any beliefs and they search for evidence with an open mind. It has been indicated that auditors might have an idea in mind or a direction but it is neither a belief nor a hypothesis, and there is no feeling of commitment to this idea or direction. Depending on this, evidence could not be classified as confirming and disconfirming. It has also been pointed out that less experienced auditors, like juniors, could not form any beliefs because all what they have to do is 'fill in forms', or in other words, their tasks are more structured and less creative. Consequently, it was suggested that carrying out the interviews with audit partners or managers would be better because it is the partner or the manager who could form a belief.

However, one of the interviewees said that he forms initial beliefs but depending on the size of the client. With small size clients, he does not form any beliefs, but with large size clients he forms initial beliefs about the financial statements. This is because with small size clients the auditor is the one who usually prepares the financial statements and then he reviews them.

---

[1] The interview schedule is included in Appendix 1.

None of the interviewees showed any confirmation bias. They all preferred to follow a balanced strategy searching for all types of evidence. It has been stated that if auditors form beliefs and then search only for confirming evidence – or for disconfirming evidence – then 'they are not doing their jobs good'.

All the interviewees agreed that expertise affects auditors' evaluation of evidence. They indicated that the more experienced the auditor is, the more efficient s/he can perform any audit task. However, their opinions about the difference between experienced and inexperienced auditors regarding evidence evaluation strategies were not clear.

Although the exploratory interviews provided some insight about audit practice and led to revising the ordering and wording of the questions, the results are very limited and could not be generalised to actual audit settings. This supported the need for conducting further interviews with practising auditors to provide more insight into the audit practice concerning the first two research questions. The findings from the interviews will help in the design of the laboratory experiment which addresses the third research question; whether there are any benefits from following the belief revision approach in audit settings.

Participants Agreement was obtained from five firms of accountants, based in the UK, to participate in the study and interviews were conducted with three partners, five senior managers and an internal auditing principal from four of the then 'Big 6' accounting firms, and a partner and two senior managers from a medium-sized firm of accountants. The level of partners and managers was chosen because the results of the pilot interviews indicated that if auditors were to form initial beliefs, this would be done by the partner or the manager. Table 4.1 includes the personal information of the interviewees.

Table 4.1 Personal information of interviewees

Interviewee	Firm size	Position in firm	Years of experience
1	Big 6	Partner	26
2	Big 6	Senior manager	10
3	Big 6	Partner	10
4	Medium	Senior manager	8
5	Medium	Senior manager	13
6	Medium	Partner	11
7	Big 6	Senior manager	11
8	Big 6	Senior manager	10
9	Big 6	Internal auditing principal	16
10	Big 6	Partner	22
11	Big 6	Senior manager	13
12	Big 6	Senior manager	13

The interview schedule was sent to the interviewees in advance[2] and the interviews were carried out in the period from November 1995 to September 1996. All the interviews were tape recorded and then transcribed.[3] Over 25 hours of interview tapes were then analysed.

Method of analysis The interviews were analysed using QSR NUD.IST[4] which is a computer package where transcriptions of interviews are entered into the programme as an on-line document and then divided into text units. Then each text unit is categorised under one or more headings, known as nodes, to create an index system. This method of analysing data has been used to arrive at conclusions related to factors affecting the process of evidence search and evaluation. These factors include source of belief, belief frame, expertise, confirmation bias, professional scepticism, diagnostic content of evidence, evidence order, evaluation mode, and time and cost.

Experimental Study

Experiments have always been used in various forms in everyday life. As people experimented in many ways to find out the best way of coping with their lives and of solving everyday problems. In the social sciences experimentation was gradually introduced in its original form first in psychology; but soon after it was adopted by sociologists and anthropologists although in various forms including natural experiments. Experiments are now useful tools in the social sciences that help in understanding human social behaviour (Sarantakos, 1993).

Field and laboratory experiments are the most popular types of experiments (Coolican, 1994). A field experiment is a study carried out in the natural environment of those studied, whilst the independent variables are manipulated by the experimenter. Other variables may well be tightly controlled but, in general, the experimenter cannot maintain the high level of control associated with the laboratory (Adams and Schvaneveldt, 1991).

Laboratory experiments are the traditional form of experimentation, which are usually referred to by writers when they talk about experiments without qualification. Their major characteristic is that they are conducted in a laboratory, where all external factors can be controlled (Sarantakos, 1993).

The laboratory research technique is the major methodology employed during the experimental process which involves comparisons of experimental and control groups under well-defined and structured conditions (Adams and Schvaneveldt, 1991).

---

[2] It should, however, be noted that some of the interviewees indicated that they did not have the time to read the interview schedule before the interview.

[3] Although the interviews were carried out individually, interviewees 11 and 12 requested to be interviewed together because of their time limit.

[4] QSR NUD.IST is an abbreviation for Non-numerical Unstructured Data Indexing and Theorizing. This computer package is useful in the analysis of qualitative data (for more information about this package see QSR NUD.IST user guide, 1995).

If the aim of the experiment is to reduce relevant extraneous variables by strict control then this is best achieved in a laboratory setting, particularly where highly accurate recordings of human cognitive functions are required (Coolican, 1994). The independent and dependent variables can be very precisely defined and accurately measured. Although the criticisms of the laboratory have been refuted in the past, recent criticism has attempted once again to suppress the use of laboratory methodologies for studying work behaviour (Dobbins et al., 1988). The main criticisms of the laboratory as a research location are narrowness of the independent and dependent variables, inability to generalise, artificiality, and using undergraduate students as subjects (Dobbins et al., 1988).

Boritz (1986) indicates that the laboratory research has dominated research into audit judgements despite criticisms that the experimental tasks were unnatural to subjects, at times biasing and lack realism as a result of structuring the experimental problems to suit the researcher's convenience. A well-conducted and meaningful laboratory study allows an investigator to make stronger statements concerning cause and effect relationships between theoretical constructs than usually can be made in field research. To some extent, the attack on the external validity of laboratory research represents a misunderstanding of the purpose of laboratory experimentation. Laboratory research should be evaluated according to the extent that it increases our understanding of the processes in work behaviour (Dobbins et al., 1988).

Laboratory experiments are often designed as true experiments (Kervin, 1992). The three most commonly true experimental designs found in business research are pretest-posttest control group design, posttest-only control group design, or factorial and blocked designs. The pretest-posttest design involves two groups formed by random assignment of cases and two measurement time points. In the posttest-only design there are two randomly assigned groups but only one measurement point following the manipulation. The factorial and blocked designs are used when there is more than one independent variable. If these other variables are manipulated, the result is a factorial design. However, if they are not manipulated, the design is said to be blocked. Factorial and blocked designs can be either pretest-posttest or posttest-only designs (Kervin, 1992).

The experimental design The main aim of the experimental study in this research is to answer the third research question which is:
- Are there any benefits from following a belief revision approach in auditing particularly benefits related to improving the efficiency and effectiveness of the audit process?

Beside this main objective, the experiment aims at answering the following questions:
- Does the change in the evidence evaluation mode affect auditors' decisions?
- Are there any differences between risk assessment and the initial belief?

These two questions are related to the factors affecting auditors' evaluation of evidence and arise as a result of the interviews' findings that will be discussed in chapters 5 and 6. Although there are other factors that still need to be considered, it was not possible to include all those factors in the design of the experiment. Other factors that could be manipulated as independent variables include belief frame and source, expertise, diagnostic content of evidence, and evidence order.

The aims of the experimental study can be achieved through a laboratory experiment with a factorial design. The form of laboratory experiments has been chosen for the following reasons:
1. It is not possible to carry out a field experiment because the interviews' findings indicated that auditors do not follow a belief revision approach in practice.
2. It is also not possible to carry out a field experiment in natural audit settings because of the time limit and the confidentiality of the audit.
3. The laboratory form of experimentation is best in investigating the cause-effect relationship between variables. As the main aim of the experiment is investigating the effect of the belief revision approach on the audit process, this can be best achieved through a laboratory experiment.

The design of the experiment is a posttest-only factorial design. The experiment is designed to include four groups with only one measurement point and two manipulated independent variables. However, the analysis is conducted between two groups at a time.

Participants Agreement was initially obtained from one of the then 'Big 6' accounting firms to provide 64 participants. The experimental instruments were sent out, in October 1997, to a co-ordinating senior manager who forwarded them to the participants, together with a letter encouraging them to participate in the experiment. However, only 16 completed experiments were received.

The co-ordinating senior manager agreed to have 40 more experiments sent to him. These were sent out in January 1998. The replies reached 29. Because this was a relatively low number to carry out the statistical analysis and because the replies were not distributed equally among the four experimental groups, agreement had to be obtained from other accounting firms to participate in the experiment.

Four other accounting firms agreed to participate in the study; three of the then 'Big 6' and one medium-sized firm. Fifty instruments were sent out in March 1998 to the four firms in proportion according to the replies already received in each of the four experimental groups. The last completed experiment was received in June 1998 making the total replies 64.

A group of partners from one of the then 'Big 6' firms also participated in the experiment and provided a 'benchmark opinion' regarding the experimental task. This 'benchmark opinion' was used as a basis to measure the effect of the belief revision approach on the effectiveness of the audit process.

The experimental task The task chosen for the experiment is assessing the materiality of the debtors item only which is a well known task to auditors.

The initial agreement obtained from one of the then 'Big 6' accounting firms was to provide year three student trainees as participants. This has been taken into consideration when designing the experimental task. Assessing the materiality of the debtors is one of the tasks that does not require much experience and, therefore, year three student trainees are not expected to have difficulty in performing the experimental task. Although higher levels of auditors participated, this was not accounted for when designing the experiment.

The simplicity of the task also helped in mitigating the experience differences between participants, hence, allowing for any differences in the results to be attributed to the independent variables.

The independent variables As the main aim of the experiment is finding out about the benefits of the belief revision approach, the evidence evaluation approach had to be considered as one of the independent variables where two approaches were manipulated; a belief revision approach and an open mind one. The difference in the approach has not been manipulated by previous auditing studies. While other studies considered the belief revision approach to be the assumed approach in audit practice, this study compares between the belief revision approach and the open mind approach in evidence evaluation. The rationale for this comparison comes from two main reasons. First, there are several indications in the previous literature that the belief revision approach is of benefit to the audit process. Second, the results of the interviews reported in chapters 5 and 6 indicated that auditors in practice follow an open mind approach in their evaluation of evidence. Hence, comparing the two approaches would help in determining whether there are any benefits from following a belief revision approach in evidence evaluation.

The belief revision approach has been operationalised through the experimental instrument by asking the participants to form an initial expectation about the materiality of the debtors after reading the background information. They were then asked to revise their expectations with pieces of evidence presented to them. Participants were not asked to provide an evaluation of pieces of evidence because under the belief revision approach it is assumed that evidence is evaluated with respect to a certain belief.

The open mind approach, on the other hand, has been operationalised in the experimental instrument so as to reflect the findings of the interviews. The results of the interviews reported in chapter 5 indicated that the first step in carrying out an audit is gathering information about the client followed by planning including the risk assessment. Hence, participants in the open mind groups were asked after being presented with the background information to conduct their initial analysis including the risk assessment. They were not asked to form any sort of initial expectations about the materiality of the debtors.

The interviewees indicated that planning and assessing risk is followed by gathering and evaluating evidence where auditors are open-minded because evidence is evaluated depending on its source and nature and not in relation to a certain belief. Participants in the experimental study were, therefore, asked to evaluate pieces of evidence presented to them without asking them to revise or form any beliefs.

The other independent variable was chosen to be the evaluation mode because its effect on auditors' decisions has not been sufficiently investigated although it might have a significant effect on the effectiveness of the audit process. There are two evidence evaluation or response modes; a SbS mode and an EoS one. Most of the previous studies employed only one response mode. Three previous studies investigated the effect of the response mode on auditors' decisions. However, the results of these studies were contradictory. Ashton and Ashton (1988) found that the response mode had an effect, while the results of Tubbs et al. (1990) and Trotman and Wright (1996) showed only a very slight effect of the response mode. Also, the results of the interviews reported in chapters 5 and 6 indicated that both response modes are employed in practice. Hence, the need for further investigation of the effect of the response mode was the rationale for choosing it as the second independent variable.

The experimental groups According to the independent variables, the experiment was divided into two main groups depending on the evidence evaluation approach; open mind or belief revision. Each group was then divided into two sub-groups according to the evidence evaluation mode; SbS or EoS. This resulted in having four experimental groups; open mind SbS, open mind EoS, belief revision SbS, and belief revision EoS. Participants were randomly assigned to one of these groups.

Description of the experimental instrument[5] The experimental instrument started with a letter to thank the auditor for his/her participation and assure the confidentiality of the experiment. Participants were then provided with two booklets; one containing the background information and pieces of evidence[6], and the other containing the answer sheets.

In the belief revision groups, participants in the SbS mode were asked to answer the questions included in the instrument. Each participant was asked to choose an initial belief about the materiality of the debtors after reading the background information. Participants had to choose a ratio ranging from 0 to 100 where 0% is very unlikely that debtors are materially correct and 100% is very likely. Participants were also asked to compare their initial belief to their risk assessment. After that, participants were presented with four pieces of mixed evidence from tests of controls and seven pieces of mixed evidence from substantive tests in a SbS mode. Each piece of evidence was presented on a separate piece of paper and participants were asked not to turn the page until they revise their belief after reading each piece of evidence. At the end, participants were asked to give their final opinion and express it as a ratio from 0 to 100, and to

---

[5] A copy of the experimental instrument for the belief revision EoS group is provided in appendix 2.
[6] The background information and pieces of evidence are adopted from two case studies by Maltby (1996); case 4 and case 7, and from pieces of evidence in Ashton and Ashton's (1988) study. However, changes and additions have been made to suit the current study.

indicate whether there is any additional work to be done and the budgeted time for this work.

Participants in the belief revision EoS group were asked to revise their belief once after reading all pieces of evidence from tests of controls presented on one piece of paper and once more after reading all pieces of evidence from substantive tests presented all on one piece of paper. As in the SbS mode, participants were asked to give their final opinion and express it as a ratio from 0 to 100, and to indicate whether there is any additional work to be done and the budgeted time for this work.

In the open mind groups, participants were asked to give their initial analysis after reading the background information and then to evaluate pieces of evidence. However, no scales were provided here for the evaluation. Participants in the open mind SbS group were provided with each piece of evidence on a separate piece of paper and were asked not to turn the page until they have written their evaluation of the evidence on the space provided in the answer sheets. Participants in the open mind EoS group were provided with evidence from tests of controls all on one piece of paper and evidence from substantive tests all on another piece of paper. Participants in both open mind groups were asked to give their final opinion in the end and express it in a percentage ranging from 0 to 100 in order to compare the results with the belief revision group. Participants were also asked to indicate whether there is any additional work needed and the budgeted time for this work.

Participants in the four experimental groups were asked to indicate their starting time after reading the background information, and their ending time after the final question relating to the budgeted time for the expected additional work needed. All participants were also asked to provide demographic information about their position, years of auditing experience, and degree subject(s) for the purpose of statistical analysis.

The group of partners who provided the 'benchmark opinion' were supplied with the experimental instrument including the background information and pieces of evidence. They were asked only to give their final opinion in the end and express it in a percentage ranging from 0 to 100, and to indicate whether there is any additional work needed and the budgeted time for this work.

Unlike other studies, the experimental design of this study included evidence from both tests of controls and substantive tests to make the task more realistic. It is also worth noting that although the experiment included mixed evidence (positive and negative) no manipulation check was included because investigating order effects was not one of the aims of the study. Participants in all the experimental groups were presented with pieces of evidence in the same order.

Pilot testing of the experiment The experiment was pilot tested by five members of academic staff, at the University of the West of England, who had previous experience in auditing. The testing resulted in changing the wording of some pieces of evidence.

The experiment was also reviewed by an audit partner and a senior manager from one of the 'Big 6' accounting firms. The following changes were made:
1. In the initial instrument, participants were told that they are required to audit the debtors to ensure that:
   - Debtors are completely and accurately stated.
   - Debtors are appropriately valued.

   However, the senior manager suggested changing this to 'You are required to audit the debtors to check whether they are materially correct'.
2. The review resulted in further changing to the wording of some pieces of evidence.
3. The initial instrument included four pieces of evidence from tests of controls and six pieces of evidence from substantive tests. The review process resulted in adding a seventh piece to evidence from substantive tests. This additional piece of evidence was considered, by the reviewing senior manager, to be rather weak positive or neutral.
4. Pieces of evidence from substantive tests were three positive and three negative. The review resulted in changing one of the negative pieces to be weak positive.
5. The four pieces of evidence from tests of controls were two positive and two negative presented in a (+ + - -) order. This order was not changed by the reviewers. However, the order of presenting the pieces of evidence from substantive tests has been changed.

Initially, the six pieces of evidence from substantive tests were three positive and three negative. They were presented in a (+ + + - - -) order. After changing one of the negative evidence to positive and adding the seventh positive evidence, the senior manager suggested changing the order of presenting the seven pieces of evidence. The change in the order of presenting the pieces of evidence depended on the nature of each piece. The reason for this change was representing what happens in reality in terms of the order by which auditors are expected to receive evidence. The change resulted in evidence being presented in a (+ + + - - + +) order.

Conclusions

This chapter presented the empirical research design of the study. The empirical study aims at finding out about the approach followed by auditors in their evaluation of evidence and whether they follow a belief revision approach and the benefits of employing such an approach. The study also aims at finding out about the factors affecting auditors' evaluation of evidence.

The data are collected depending personal interviews and a laboratory experiment. Personal semi-structured interviews are employed to provide some insight about the audit practice concerning evidence evaluation approaches, and factors affecting this process.

A laboratory experiment is employed for collecting data that will help in comparing the belief revision approach with the approach auditors normally follow in practice which is referred to as the open mind approach. The data will also help in determining the effect of the response mode on auditors' decisions and comparing between risk assessment and the initial belief. The experiment included four groups depending on the evidence evaluation approach and evaluation mode. The experimental task was auditing the debtors to check whether they are materially correct.

The results and analyses of data collected from the interviews and experiments are presented in the following three chapters.

Chapter 5

Results of Interviews: Auditors' Approaches in Evaluating Evidence

Introduction

The aim of this chapter is to present the results of the interviews with regards to the evidence evaluation approach employed by auditors in practice. This is done with the aim to find out whether auditors follow a belief revision approach in their evaluation of evidence, and if not, what is/are the approach/s followed by them.

The following points are addressed in this chapter:
- The evidence evaluation approach followed by auditors.
- The evidence evaluation approach in case of new vs. continuing clients.
- The evidence evaluation approach in case of small vs. large clients.

The Evidence Evaluation Approach Followed by Auditors

The audit process, in its simple form, involves planning, collecting and evaluating evidence, and forming the final opinion.

Most of the interviewees presented the audit process by talking about the sequence of the steps of performing an audit. There was no difference between the interviewees regarding the main steps of the audit process. One of the interviewees presented the audit process by talking about work done by different levels of auditors. He indicated that after planning and risk assessment, there is work done by staff including evidence search and evaluation. This is followed by reviewing the work by the audit manager. Then the work is reviewed by the partner. In the end the audit team meets to clear up certain issues that might have arisen and come to a final opinion.

The results of the interviews indicated that auditors in practice follow what they referred to as the 'open mind' approach in their evaluation of evidence. This is evidenced from the following quotes:

> We will gather the evidence with an open mind and then come back and produce the opinion. I don't think there is any point of time while we gather evidence we say that supports and that doesn't. It is not a balance (2: 29)[1].

> We're starting with an open mind, or barely we got a slight bias because obviously we want him as a client (12: 66).

> You don't have any prejudice before you start work (1: 9).

Although the interviewees indicated that the initial belief might be risk assessment, an idea, assumption or expectation, they still preferred to be open-minded during their search for evidence. This was obvious when they were asked about their commitment to what they might consider as an initial belief. The main result here was that there would not be any commitment to the initial belief whatever it was.

If auditors subsequently find that they need to change their opinion they do and 'there is no real pressure to move away from it' (2: 27). However, the importance of the initial assumption or opinion is that the audit plan comes out of it.

> The decision process is not quite as you say. The initial opinion is really a basis on which someone can plan but it is not something you are particularly committed to (2: 31).

Accordingly, evidence is not classified to confirming and disconfirming. If there was evidence coming through to say that auditors were right to be concerned about a certain area of risk, then that might affect the formation of the final opinion. But it is not commitment. 'I feel basically neutral. I mean it doesn't really matter to me what opinion we come to. The fact is that we want to be right' (5: 20).

Furthermore, auditors would not be sure when they would start forming an initial belief or hypothesis.

> We're actually struggling as to when the hypothesis kicks in because of, when we get down to doing the audit that's when we've got a whole lot of stuff already whether it'll be proposed back with a hypothesis in my mind or not (12: 69).

The view that the initial belief was mostly considered to be the risk assessment eliminated the feeling of commitment to it. Consequently, evidence is not classified to confirming and disconfirming. If, for example, auditors assessed an item as being of high risk, and then they find evidence to tell that there is something wrong, they do feel that they were right to consider this item to be of high risk. But this is different from commitment.

Auditors also might not feel committed to their risk assessment because 'the basis on which you make those assessments is always that this is preliminary and that it may not be supported by later evidence which comes to light' (7: 32).

---

[1] The numbers between brackets refer to the number of the interviewee followed by the number(s) of the paragraph(s) from which the quote is taken.

The term commitment to the auditors does not mean ending up with the same opinion and it does not mean classifying evidence to confirming and disconfirming. Commitment means following an issue through to the end.

> Yes probably we are committed to it [initial belief] because as soon as we identify that there is something that we need to look at we have to follow it through to the end. It doesn't mean that we have to end up with the same opinion (3: 18).

One of the interviewees indicated that the initial belief or expectation is not formed by the audit team, it is formed by each auditor on his own. 'It is an expectation in my own mind' (4: 16). He also said that he is not committed to his expectations in any way, even if he finds evidence supporting it. This highlights an important issue concerning employing a belief revision behaviour unconsciously. In other words, auditors might seem to be following an open mind approach where no prior beliefs affect their evaluation of evidence. However, they are unconsciously or implicitly following a belief revision approach where there are some beliefs or expectations in their mind. Consequently, this might affect their evaluation of evidence. The significant effect of this issue is that when auditors do not admit forming initial beliefs, studying the effects of these beliefs on evidence evaluation would not be an easy task especially that there many other factors that interact to affect auditors' attitudes toward evidence.

A different view was expressed by another interviewee who indicated that the initial opinion is formed by the partner or the manager during the planning stage and this initial opinion would be updated after viewing the work done by the staff. However, the interviewee added that he does not see that forming an initial opinion has got such significance. He said that it is not likely to issue a qualified report because 'the reality is that sort of clients that we deal with, a qualified opinion is not really an option' (10: 12). He also added that they would not approach an audit 'from a proposition that we're to disapprove' (10: 87).

The view that the initial opinion would be formed by the partner or the manager might imply that partners or managers would follow a belief revision approach while the other audit staff are more likely to follow an open mind one. The important point here is whether the partner or the manager expresses his/her initial opinion to the staff. If this happens, some motivational factors might affect the staff's work. In particular, a staff auditor might try to create a good picture of him/herself by pleasing the partner or the manager. This might be done by trying to collect evidence confirming the partner's or manager's initial opinion and ignoring any disconfirming evidence. If this happened it would have significant effects on the effectiveness of the audit process.

The previous analysis of the interviews revealed that auditors do not want to be described as belief revisers even if they have initial beliefs. Belief revision, according to the interviewees' views, is a very systematic way in evaluating audit evidence. The previous studies did not address the question of whether auditors follow this behaviour in practice. Most studies focused on investigating the validity of the predictions of the belief-adjustment model without trying to find out whether this model is valid in itself as a method of explaining auditors' behaviour in practice. This mainly might be due to the underlying assumption that auditors form an initial belief in practice.

Church (1990) argues that auditors often inherit or generate beliefs to guide their search for evidence. He claims that diagnostic beliefs guiding the collection and evaluation of evidence could be formulated from prior year's working papers. It has also been argued that auditors' search for evidence is influenced by an explicitly or implicitly formulated belief, particularly during analytical review and in judgement tasks like evaluating internal controls and assessing audit risk (Libby, 1981 and 1985).

Although the previous literature did not investigate the validity of the belief revision approach in describing auditors' behaviour during their evaluation of evidence, some studies argue about the importance of following such an approach. Peters (1990) indicated that the formation of beliefs helps auditors in focusing their evidence search and evaluation, thus making the process more tractable. Hogarth and Einhorn (1992) claim that following a belief revision approach with the sequential processing of evidence can reduce memory load.

Bedard and Biggs (1991) indicated that the existence of the American SAS 56 on analytical procedures is the reason why auditors form an initial belief and then search for evidence to prove or deny it. The SAS 56 calls for auditors to hypothesise likely causes of material changes in the financial statements and to develop plans to investigate the formulated beliefs. However, this statement applies only to the analytical procedures and not to the entire audit process. Bedard and Biggs (1991) argue that SAS 56 is emphasised in the Hogarth and Einhorn theory of decision making. It should be noted here that analytical review procedure, as a type of evidence, is different from other types of evidence because it involves investigating relationships between different components of the financial statements and also the effect of external factors on the financial statements. This sort of investigation is made to obtain predictions that can then be compared to the reported figures (Spicer and Oppenheim et al., 1990). Thus, an essential characteristic of analytical review is that it involves making predictions, which could be considered as the initial beliefs, and would fit into the belief-adjustment model. However, not all methods of obtaining audit evidence would involve making predictions.

The conclusion is that in practice auditors' evidence evaluation would follow an open mind approach rather than a belief revision one. Figures 5.1 and 5.2 will help in differentiating between the two approaches.

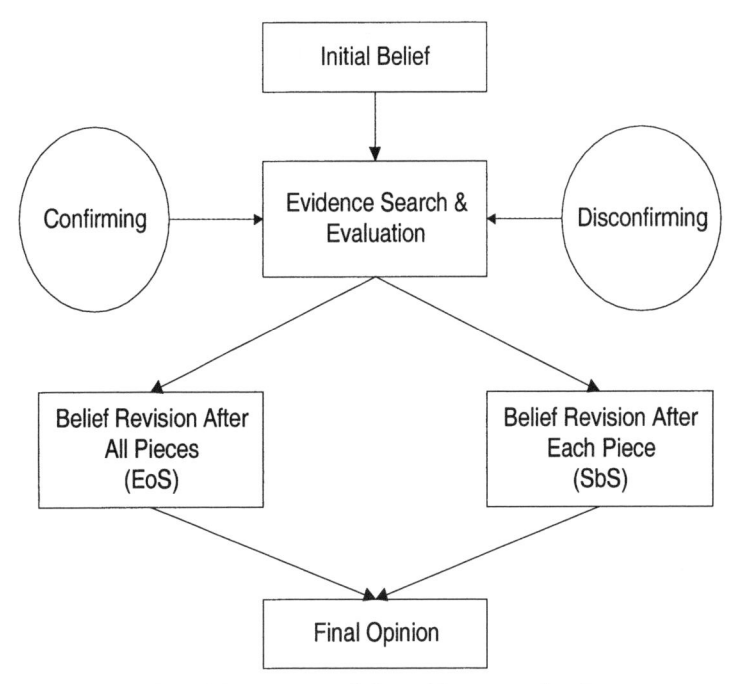

```
                    ┌──────────────┐
                    │Initial Belief│
                    └──────┬───────┘
                           ▼
   ╭─────────╮      ┌──────────────┐      ╭──────────────╮
   │Confirming│────▶│Evidence Search&│◀────│ Disconfirming│
   ╰─────────╯      │  Evaluation  │      ╰──────────────╯
                    └──────┬───────┘
              ┌────────────┴────────────┐
              ▼                         ▼
   ┌────────────────────┐    ┌────────────────────┐
   │Belief Revision After│    │Belief Revision After│
   │    All Pieces      │    │    Each Piece      │
   │       (EoS)        │    │       (SbS)        │
   └──────────┬─────────┘    └──────────┬─────────┘
              └────────────┬────────────┘
                           ▼
                    ┌──────────────┐
                    │ Final Opinion│
                    └──────────────┘
```

Figure 5.1 The belief revision approach in evidence evaluation

Figure 5.1 illustrates the belief revision approach in evidence search and evaluation. The belief revision approach is based on two main assumptions. First, an initial belief is formed and revised according to pieces of evidence received. The initial belief could take the form of a likelihood assessment, or it could take the form of an expected cause of fluctuation.[2] The revision of the initial belief could be done in one of two modes. In an SbS mode, the belief is revised after evaluating each pieces of evidence. In an EoS mode, the belief is revised once after receiving and evaluating all pieces of evidence.

The second assumption of the belief revision approach is that evidence is considered with respect to its relation with the current belief. Previous studies in the area of belief revision were always concerned with auditors' attitudes toward evidence as confirming or disconfirming to their beliefs.

---

[2] These are the forms of beliefs included in the previous auditing studies in the area of belief revision.

```
        ┌──────────────┐
        │ Initial Belief│
        └──────┬───────┘
               │
               ▼
  ╭─────╮   ┌─────────────────┐   ╭──────╮
  │Source│──▶│ Evidence Search &│◀──│Nature│
  ╰─────╯   │   Evaluation    │   ╰──────╯
            └────────┬────────┘
                     │
                     ▼
            ┌──────────────┐
            │ Final Opinion│
            └──────────────┘
```

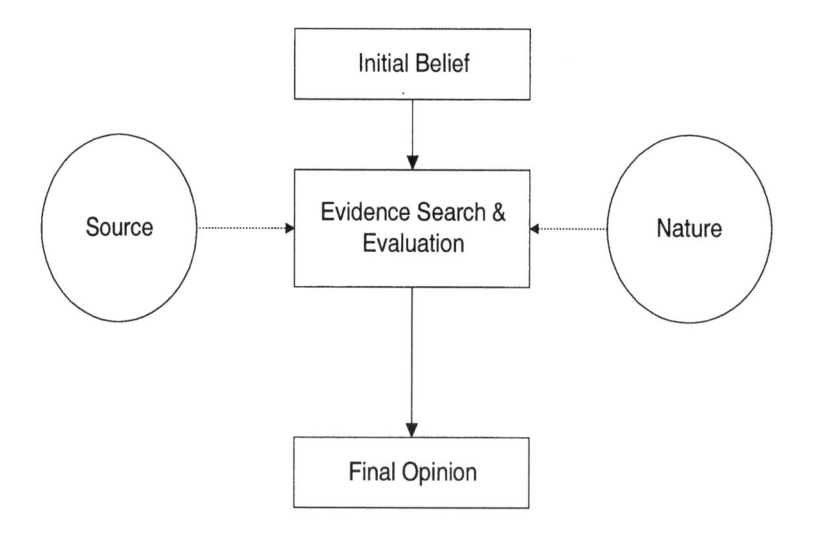

Figure 5.2 The open mind approach in evidence evaluation

On the other hand, the open mind approach, as shown in Figure 5.2 depends on evaluating evidence according to its nature and source. In following an open mind approach, the auditors would still have an initial belief before starting their search for and evaluation of evidence as evidenced from the interviews. However, the nature of this initial belief is debatable. The main finding of the interviews is that this initial belief would be the risk assessment. There are two main differences between the open mind and the belief revision approach. First, the open mind approach does not involve the process of updating the belief with current pieces of evidence. Second, evidence in the open mind approach is not evaluated in relation to any prior beliefs. Auditors do not view evidence as confirming or disconfirming a certain belief.

It is worth noting that following a belief revision approach does not mean ignoring the source and nature of evidence. In fact, the strength of evidence would always depend on its source and nature. However, previous auditing studies in the area of belief revision were more concerned with studying the factors affecting auditors' attitudes toward confirming and disconfirming evidence which might not hold true in the actual audit settings.

An interesting and important point that one of the interviewed partners raised was that there is a difference in the audit approaches between the US and the UK. This is mainly because of the difference in the idea about the audit process. He indicated that the American idea is that the audit is a linear process but it's not. He stated that:

... the American idea that the audit is a linear process but it's not. You know, the audit is not a linear process. The audit is an iterative process (10: 96).

This means that auditing in practice could not be approached adopting a belief revision behaviour which is a very systematic approach. However, one has to be sceptical about such an argument because the audit process does not differ from one country to another. There might be some differences in the auditing standards, but whether this will affect auditors' behaviour in evaluating evidence is an area that needs further research.

The Evidence Evaluation Approach in Case of New vs. Continuing Clients

The analysis of the interviews revealed that the audit steps are the same for both new and continuing clients. The difference is that with continuing clients more time is needed at the start of the audit to gather information about the client and the business. This is evidenced from the following quotes:

> ...with new clients you have to spend more time before planning the work. You have to collect some information about the client. You have to spend more time on assessing the areas of risk ... How long company has been a client, I think there might be a relationship here because having people around for sometime can result in better identifications of any problems. With a new client it can be quite difficult to get things set up (1: 13, 17).
> Obviously what we are doing in each step will change for each client. So the principal steps are the same but the work which is done in each step will vary (2: 8).

> The main steps are still there. There is only a slight difference. If it is a new client there is more work to be done specially at the beginning to collect more information about the client (4: 8).

> The only difference I suppose with a new client is starting. I mean gathering knowledge about the client's business is longer, I mean it takes much more time than with a continuing client. But all the steps are the same ... I suppose the longer the company has been a client the more you are familiar with (6: 8, 14).

> I usually have a very very sceptical view of new clients. That's absolutely why I'm searching for evidence to make sure that I'm not taking on risk that I'm not aware of. I guess with existing clients where you had many years of contact, I think perhaps it's slightly less cynical (11: 9).

It is, therefore, clear that the audit process will take longer time in case of new clients compared to continuing ones. This is the reason that with new clients the audit fee is higher in the first year.

The most important issue raised by the interviewees in relation to how long company has been a client was the effect that this might have on the formation of ideas, expectations, assumptions, or risk assessment. The following quotes illustrate the opinions of the interviewees:

> If it is a continuing client one will have knowledge of what they do. So you do have a better understanding. But opinion is a strong word ... You have an idea of what is happening but it is not formal. At the planning process we put an assumption based on our previous knowledge as to whether the controls are good. We test the controls and we have to change our opinion if they are not good. So yes we do have an idea (2: 12, 14).

> ... in terms of forming an initial risk assessment for financial statements, your experience of the client and how competent they are, how accurate their accounts proved to be in the past, whether we found lots of material errors or control problems, that would form part of the risk assessment. So those types of global facts, if you like, would be taken into account as well as the more specific factors addressing the individual financial statement components (7: 26).

> ...By building relationships with the client we can actually say we have yes in mind a figure. I think generally speaking, perhaps the more you know the client, the more you can form initial assumptions. I guess so ... Yes, you do have a better idea, a better understanding. Having said that, if you have a client for a long time, it would be easier to form your initial assumptions (9: 12, 18).

> I think, I mean maybe if I just, through my thinking on say my major clients, my initial sort of hypothesis, I guess, will probably be based on number of years of experience of working with this client and I would have had a number of influences of how, what is the overall riskiness of the business. If it's a generally high risk industry, what are the motivations of the management, and just generally what are the levels of the systems. I think I would build up sort of an initial view as to what you would expect by a client doing, if you like, with its financial statements (11: 15).

The importance of the interviewees' opinions about the differences between new and continuing clients is that it affects the employment of the belief revision approach. Specifically, how long a company has been a client might have an effect on the timing of forming an initial belief whether this belief is risk assessment or any other sort of ideas, assumptions, and expectations. From the quotes given above, it could be concluded that the formation of initial beliefs would be easier for continuing than for new clients. In addition, the initial beliefs in the case of continuing clients could be formed at an earlier stage than in the case of new clients. The following quote sums up the previous conclusion:

> If it is a new client we can try to identify these areas [risky areas] either through our experience of other companies in the same industry or through discussions with the management ... With a continuing client we can form our initial opinion at the beginning depending on our previous knowledge. With a new client I think it is difficult to form an initial opinion from the beginning. It might take a longer time to start forming your opinion (3: 8, 10).

In addition, the nature of the initial belief would be based on the number of years of experience of working with a client.

> I think two clients I have at the moment, very well I would most definitely start with hypothesis that the accounts will be right. So when we are doing, we are basically gathering evidence really to make sure that they are right, to know that we haven't been sort of cheated or tripped and the areas of judgement are reasonable judgements. I have another client where I start with a hypothesis I know what they'll produce will be totally wrong, absolutely totally wrong. You could actually ask yourself well there's a bigger question here, should they remain a client? Well commercially actually they are actually an extremely good client because we do huge amounts of work for them. But it's a very different, you know, sort of starting point. It's a starting point that says I am going to pull everything apart. It will, indeed I'll assume everything is wrong (11: 51).

The Evidence Evaluation Approach in Case of Small vs. Large Clients

Unlike how long a company has been a client, most of the interviewees did not regard size of client as a factor that might affect the formation of their initial beliefs. When the interviewees were asked about the effect that the size of a client might have on their initial beliefs, the following were some of their answers:

> Size of client no, but larger clients tend to be better organised because they have the resources, and I think that's all. But the assumption is not based on the size (2: 17).

> Size of client, I don't think size is of importance. I necessarily, I mean it depends on the control systems. The only point is that with larger clients you are expecting to have well established control systems, so you can rely more on these systems. That's it (6: 14).

> Size of client, I don't think. The client is a client whatever his size is. Any client is expecting to get a full service (9: 16).

Although the interviewees regarded size of client as an irrelevant factor, they agreed that it would affect their reliance on the internal controls. However, one of the interviewees indicated that in case of large clients the reliance on the internal controls might have a bad effect if these controls went wrong.

> Size of client is relevant. The large clients will often have better systems but if it went wrong the downside could be much greater. So it would depend very much on the client circumstances as to how you form your initial opinion (5: 12).

It is also worth noting that because the interviewees deal mainly with large clients, size might not be one of the factors that they would consider. This point has been made clear as follows:

Probably you put this to the wrong person because I don't deal with small companies. But the size of the client would affect us because I think the smaller the client the less internal control there is (10: 24).

An important issue raised by one of the interviewees was that the difference in the audit approaches between the US and the UK is a factor of the size of clients. The interviewee indicated that the types of audit that occur in the US are completely different than the types of audit that occur in the UK, and research in the US is based mainly on small firms. He stated that:

> ... the types of audit that occur there [US], they are completely different to the types of audit that occur here [UK]. They do the research, lot of research that I've seen in America is based on small firms. We are auditing small companies but ... it might be that it's a bank appointed auditor, you know it's very different (10: 70).

The previous opinion about the difference between the types of audits in the US and the UK is based on auditing research. However, auditing research might not reflect the reality. Most of the US auditing research depends on laboratory experiments and, even though, this type of experimentation is useful in investigating the cause-effect relationship between variables, it might not be reflective of the real practice. In addition, most of the US auditing research in the area of belief revision was conducted in large accounting firms.

Conclusions

This chapter focused on reporting the results of the interviews carried out with 12 experienced auditors with regards to the audit approach employed with the aim to find out whether auditors follow a belief revision approach in their evaluation of evidence.

The analysis of the interviews indicated that in practice auditors follow an open mind approach in their evaluation of evidence. However, one could not ignore the fact that the answers of the interviewees indicated that there is, to some extent, an initial belief and this belief is easier to form in case of continuing clients rather than new ones. This initial belief could take the form of risk assessment, a clean initial opinion, an assumption, or an expectation, but there would always be a basis for collecting and evaluating evidence. These sorts of beliefs are different from the beliefs referred to in the previous literature which took the form of an initial likelihood assessment or an expected cause of fluctuation.

There are two main differences between the open mind approach referred to by the interviewees and the belief revision approach. First, the open mind approach does not involve the systematic revision of beliefs with pieces of evidence received. Second, evidence in the open mind approach is not classified to confirming and disconfirming with relation to a certain belief.

Chapter 6

Results of Interviews: Factors Affecting Auditors' Evaluation of Evidence

Introduction

This chapter is concerned with analysing the interviews with respect to the factors affecting auditors' evaluation of evidence. The factors discussed with the interviewees are those referred to by previous auditing studies about the belief revision approach and the belief-adjustment model. In addition, a discussion of the effect of time and cost on auditors' search for evidence is also included. This issue is important because it relates to the efficiency of the audit process.

The following points are addressed in this chapter:
- Formation of the initial belief including its meaning, source, and frame.
- Expertise.
- Confirmation bias.
- Professional scepticism and conservatism.
- Diagnostic content of evidence.
- Evidence order.
- Evaluation mode.
- Time and cost.

Formation of the Initial Belief

The formation of the auditor's initial beliefs incorporates two main factors; the source of the belief, and its frame (Church, 1990; and McMillan and White, 1993). In addition, the discussion of the results of the interviews in the previous chapter revealed that there is no agreement between auditors as to the meaning of the initial belief. Thus, the analysis of the formation of the initial belief would focus on three factors; concept of the initial belief, source of belief, and belief frame.

Concept of the Initial Belief

The interview schedule started with a question about the main steps of the audit process. The purpose of this question was to find out whether the interviewees would mention anything about forming an initial belief without leading them to the answer. However, none of them stated voluntarily that at any stage of the audit an initial belief is formed. The interviewees were, therefore, asked directly about forming an initial belief. The word initial opinion was used instead of initial belief or hypothesis because it is not a technical word and the word 'opinion' is in more common usage in auditing circles. However, one of the interviewees commented on the inappropriateness of the word as it is a 'strong word'. Each interviewee used his/her own wording to express what s/he viewed to be an initial opinion.

Most interviewees considered risk assessment to be their initial belief. Others indicated that the initial belief might be an idea, expectation, assumption, or a clean initial opinion.

Belief or hypothesis Previous studies in the area of belief revision used the words belief and hypothesis to refer to the same concept. Some studies used the word belief (for example Ashton and Ashton, 1988; and Tubbs et al., 1990), while others used the word hypothesis (for example Marchant, 1989; Kida, 1984; and Ismail and Trotman, 1995). Furthermore, Bamber et al. (1997) used the two words interchangeably in their study and Messier and Plumlee (1987) used the words beliefs, assumptions and anticipation. Messier and Plumlee (1987, p. 349) stated that:

> Beliefs formed and assumptions made in the initial phase of the audit determine anticipation of an error-type. Such anticipation should influence the procedures chosen for substantive tests and interpretation of the results of those tests.

They indicated that the auditor's perception of the client's internal control system would help in retrieving a 'schema' from the auditor's memory that 'guides inferences regarding the types of errors the system will produce and the audit procedures that will allow the impact of those error-types to be assessed' (Messier and Plumlee, 1987, p. 350). This concept of an assumption or anticipation implies that it is a negative one where the auditor anticipates a condition not favouring the client. However, this is not always the case as the previous studies indicated that the initial belief could be a positive or a negative one.

Hogarth and Einhorn (1992) used the words current belief, hypothesis and current opinion, but no specific definitions were mentioned about each of these terms. The only implicit differentiation they made was referring to the degree of belief in the initial hypothesis. This degree is the strength of the initial hypothesis. In other words, it is the degree auditors believe that, for example, debtors are likely to be overstated or even fairly stated. Thus, one can arrive at a conclusion that the belief is the strength of the hypothesis. However, no such distinction was considered by previous studies. Hypothesis generation itself has been defined as 'the process of developing a proposal about an underlying event or principle that explains a recognised pattern of data' (Bedard and Biggs, 1991, p. 624).

Although the words idea, expectation and assumption were used by the interviewees, none of them gave a specific definition to these words. Furthermore, one of the interviewees used the words assumption, opinion and idea interchangeably. He said:

> You have an **idea** of what is happening but it is not formal. At the planning process we put an **assumption** based on our previous knowledge as to whether the controls are good. We test the controls and we have to change our **opinion** if they are not good. So yes we do have an **idea** (2: 14).

The term initial belief has also been used to refer to the initial assessment of material error (McMillan and White, 1996), thus, putting the concept of materiality in the way. None of the interviewees referred to materiality as a factor in forming the initial belief, although it has been stated that setting off materiality levels is carried out during the planning stage.

Although the agreement on a specific term to be used is of great importance, more important is the interpretation of that term. The following discussion focuses on two main concepts of the initial belief as they have been raised by the interviewees.

Risk assessment as the initial belief Most interviewees seemed to regard their *ideas, expectations, assumptions* or *risk assessment* as their initial opinion of whether the financial statements are true and fair. And even though the words idea, expectation and assumption were used by the interviewees, their strongest view was considering risk assessment to be the initial belief.

> The point I am trying to indicate to you is that what you are doing is trying to assess risk and then plan your audit before the statements are there. So you don't have any prejudice before you start work (1: 9).

> Yep, we form an initial opinion. It is our risk assessment. I think the risk assessment is an initial opinion because it is telling us what areas are of high risk, what areas need to be focused on (6: 10).

This view is consistent with the UK standard 400.2 which states that audit evidence from tests of control is collected to support the assessed level of control risk.

Examples of initial beliefs, as indicated in the previous studies, are that 'debtors are likely to be overstated', 'debtors are likely to be collected' or 'creditors are likely to be understated'. The results of the interviews indicated that risk assessment is not the same as the previous beliefs. It has been stated that:

> Risk assessment, I would say, is more looking at debtors and saying is there anything about this business that we know that means if they're likely to get their debtors wrong or not ...It doesn't mean we're assuming from the start that there is an error there, that the amount would be wrong, but it's something that we'd obviously pay attention to

during the audit. So the two are quite linked. I guess we're really defining risk as being the risk of there is a misstatement but I wouldn't say that a misstatement under a risk is the same thing (7: 12).

...I don't think it's as simple to say that debtors may be overstated. In a number of cases the issues may be more technical ...so you might not say debtors will be overstated, you might say X has not got a very good grasp of this area, you will need to look at it further (8: 10).
... I don't think we can relate that to whether we think the financial statements are fairly stated or not. It's where we think we're going to focus our efforts in order to be able to give an unqualified opinion. So it's where we think we need to focus. If we think that a company has got high area of risk, it doesn't mean that we think that the accounts are untrue or fair. So we assume that the accounts are fairly stated because we would assume that the controls are operating effectively. It's just that we would, you know that's where we would concentrate our efforts (10: 16).

It has also been stated that risk assessment is

focusing us upon things which we wanted to be sure about. So for example if you've got a property industry client where there have been a lot of problems over the last few years, you're going to focus upon property valuations (5: 10).

In the auditing literature, audit risk hypothesis generation has been defined as 'that part of the audit-planning process in which auditors identify potential audit risks as a first step in developing an audit plan designed, in part, to mitigate those risks' (Peters, 1990, p. 84). Audit risks include inherent risk, control risk and detection risk. While inherent risk means the probability of occurrence of a material error before the operation of internal control procedures, control risk is the probability of not preventing or detecting a material error by the internal control systems. Detection risk, on the other hand, is the probability of failure of audit procedures to detect a material error in the financial statements. The three components of audit risk are all integrated into the overall audit risk which is the risk that there is a material error in the financial statements after completing the audit and issuing an unqualified opinion (Spicer and Oppenheim et al., 1990).

However, risk assessment referred to by the interviewees was not that sort of assessment, which involves assessing the different components of audit risk, and which Spicer and Oppenheim et al. (1990, p. 91) refer to as assessment at the account balance or class-of-transactions level. Rather, risk assessment referred to by the interviewees implied a preliminary assessment made at an overall level during the planning in which risk is assessed as either high, medium or low taking into consideration the environment and other circumstances the business is operating within.

Ricchiute (1992) indicated that in practice, auditors might combine inherent and control risk in a single inherent/control risk assessment. He also added that practically audit risk is often judged subjectively as being high, medium, or low because inherent, control, and detection risks are often difficult to quantify. However, if they could be quantified, the audit risk for a particular account is measured using the audit risk model:

Audit Risk (AR) = Inherent Risk (IR) × Control Risk (CR) × Detection Risk (DR)

The results of the interviews support what has been indicated by Ricchiute (1992) in that risk is often assessed subjectively as being high, medium, or low without a clear differentiation between its components. This result indicates the gap between audit practice and the literature. It also indicates the gap between audit practice and the audit standards. The audit literature and audit standards describe risk assessment in a very systematic manner where auditors assess inherent risk, control risk, and detection risk. On the other hand, risk assessment in practice does not always proceed in this systematic manner. To illustrate this, it might be relevant to consider the UK auditing standards related to risk assessment. Risk assessment is governed by SAS 300.

SAS 300.1(b) (APB, 1995) states that 'Auditors should use professional judgment to assess the components of audit risk and to design audit procedures to ensure it is reduced to an acceptably low level'. The components of audit risk are inherent risk, control risk, and detection risk.

SAS 300.2 (APB, 1995) is concerned with inherent risk and states that 'In developing their audit approach and detailed procedures, auditors should assess inherent risk in relation to financial statement assertions about material account balances and classes of transaction, taking account of factors relevant both to the entity as a whole and to the specific assertions'.

SAS 300.4 (APB, 1995) on control risk states that 'If auditors, after obtaining an understanding of the accounting system and control environment, expect to be able to rely on their assessment of control risk to reduce the extent of their substantive procedures, they should make a preliminary assessment of control risk for material financial statement assertions, and should plan and perform tests of control to support that assessment'.

SAS 300.7 (APB, 1995) on detection risk states that 'Auditors should consider the assessed levels of inherent and control risk in determining the nature, timing and extent of substantive procedures required to reduce audit risk to an acceptable level'.

The previous auditing standards raise two main issues. First, while the standards provide with a systematic description of risk assessment, the practice does not follow this systematic approach is assessing risk. The differentiation between the components of risk in practice is not always clear-cut. Second, risk assessment could not be viewed as an initial belief which is updated or revised with pieces of evidence received until a final opinion is reached. Rather, risk assessment is only a basis on which auditors can plan their extent of work. Although the explanations provided with SAS 300 indicate that auditors may revise their assessment of the components of audit risk during the course of an audit, this revision is different from the revision of beliefs described in the belief revision approach. The revision of risk assessment would result in modifying the planned substantive procedures but not a revision of an opinion. In addition, risk assessment is only revised if information comes to the auditors' attention that differs significantly from the information on which they originally assessed inherent and control risks (APB, 1995, SAS 300, para 55).

Turley and Cooper (1991) indicate that the application of risk concepts is a major development in audit methodology in the UK in the last decade. The application of risk concepts can help provide a structure for evidence collection by determining the direction and quantity of evidence needed. However, it could not be concluded from the results of the interviews that risk assessment is valid in itself to be the initial belief. The underlying assumption of the initial belief is that it is something that could be revised or updated with subsequent pieces of evidence. However, the interviewees indicated that risk assessment is not revisable. It has been stated, in the interviews, that if , for example, an area is assessed to be of high risk, the evidence collected whether it is confirming or disconfirming would not deny the fact that this area is of high risk.

A clean opinion as the initial belief The other view was that if auditors were to follow a belief revision strategy, then they have to start with a clean opinion as their initial belief.

> It is difficult to say at what stage you form your initial opinion. So it is probably right to say that you will expect to give a clean opinion and do not know yet where to qualify your opinion. What you have is what is called a planning document, and no audit is the same as another audit. The chap who is issuing the opinion at the top has got to have very clear ideas (1: 15).

Auditors in an accounting firm, especially if it is a big one, would not accept a client if they think that they would give a qualified opinion. This view is consistent with what Mautz and Sharaf (1961) said in that the financial statement assertions should be considered as the initial beliefs or hypotheses to start with. In this case the financial statement assertions will be regarded by auditors as correct figures to start with which is a clean opinion. Mautz and Sharaf (1961, p. 109) argued that the auditor

> must school himself to see assertions in the financial statements as nothing more than hypotheses until he has determined the kind and extent of evidence he will need to arrive at a judgement, has obtained the evidence, and subjected it to critical review. Only then is he ready to permit that evidence to work upon his mind and lead him either to accept or deny the assertion before him or to decide that with the evidence available he cannot reach a rational judgment.

This view is also consistent with the UK auditing standard SAS 400.3 which states that audit evidence from substantive procedures together with any evidence from tests of controls is collected to support the relevant financial statement assertions. Knechel and Messier (1990) support this view. They indicated that the audit is a judgement process that involves two interrelated actions. 'First, the auditor must choose which evidence to examine relative to an audit assertion. Second, the evidence chosen must be evaluated with respect to that audit assertion' (Knechel and Messier, 1990, p. 388).

Starting with a clean initial opinion would provide with an objective basis for evidence search and evaluation, however, it might not help in pointing the attention toward any problematic areas in the accounts. This issue is emphasised in the case of analytical review where there might be changes in the accounts, in which case the formation of expectations about the reasons for these changes would help in guiding the process of evidence search.

Sources of Beliefs

Beliefs could either be generated by the auditors themselves or inherited. Sources of inherited beliefs include the client personnel, auditor's superiors, decision aids, or pervious years' working papers (Church, 1990; and Church and Schneider, 1993).

By looking at the results of the interviews, the overwhelming conclusion is that any opinion is formulated by the audit team altogether.

> We work very much as a team. The whole team plans the process and the idea itself comes out as a result of discussions and suggestions from every individual member of the audit team(2: 19).
> As a team. The partner, manager, staff. We all work together. We meet together to discuss. I mean we do the planning together, and risk is assessed as a result of putting our opinions together (6: 16).
> We very much work as a team. Within the planning process we work as a team. There are supervisors as well, but we all go through the process. The manager then looks at the work. Then finally finish up with the partner who looks at issues which the manager highlights (9: 20).

It has also been claimed that any opinion is formulated by the audit team particularly if it is a qualified opinion.

> I think it is rare that you formulate an opinion on your own particularly if it is a qualified opinion. So I would say that the opinion is formulated by a team (1: 19).

And in the case of large clients that big accounting firms deal with, it might not be the whole team together in every audit task because the number of auditors involved in one audit is huge.

> As a team. Yeah, well it might not be a full team. I mean we're talking about the sort of companies that I work on. Teams are huge, so we would have, we might have in one audit, you might have four or five partners and half a dozen senior managers and many staff. So it wouldn't be a solo effort. It would be a team basis but the composition of the team wouldn't be the full audit team because you would never have space to put them in (10: 26).

The only exception to the team approach would be the case of a sole practitioner.

> I think the approach is very much on a team effort, and the only exception would be if you were a sole practitioner (12: 80).

However, there was an argument that even though the work is done as a team but the initial opinion would be formed by the partner or the manager at the planning stage.

> ...it would primarily be the partner or the manager at the planning stage and then obviously your view won't change very much until the point when you come to view the work done by the staff (5: 14).

Thus, the view of the partner or the manager would not change very much until the point when s/he reviews the work done by the staff. Furthermore, it has been claimed that basically the initial assessment would be formed by the audit manager who would then discuss it with the audit partner.

> ...What would happen is probably the audit manager would form initial assessment. He would then discuss that with the audit partner to see [what he would] agree at. And then the audit team would then actually do work to confirm or to amend those assessments and they're doing some more detailed work. So it's very much a team effort (7: 30).

It has also been argued that source of the initial belief would depend on the client. If a client is perceived to be comparatively straight-forward, then most of the risk assessment would be done by the senior manager, brief conversation with the partner involved. However, if an audit is perceived to be more risky, it becomes necessary to talk to other specialists throughout the rest of the firm.

Decision aids like expert systems or decision support systems did not prove to be a source of auditors' beliefs. Such systems are not cost effective, so accounting firms would not rely on them because it is a cost/benefit exercise. It has been commented that:

> No, but there is research going on about this point and I don't think any of the accounting firms are using these systems now (1: 21).

It has also been stated that accounting firms use the technology of the computer, but not in forming assumptions or opinions.

> ...It is something which has been brought in. In fact there is one about the audit process which is being tested at the moment. So that's something, to be honest, is a question of a year's time. But at the moment it's fairly experience basis rather than any sort of computer package or formula that get followed. So we don't specifically use such systems in the opinion formation. I mean we obviously use various computer testing techniques but that's just part of getting information. It may be in the form of sample selection, but in terms of assessing risk no (5: 16).

...The opinion is our opinion. We don't have a computer system that says OK. But we have some programs that you would use. So we use the technology of the computer, but not in forming our assumptions or opinions (9: 22).

The previous view about the use of decision aids in forming initial beliefs might limit, at least in the meantime, the consideration of Kaplan et al.'s (1992) suggestion about the benefits of using such decision aids in providing explanations for changes discovered in an analytical review.

The implication of the results of the interviews concerning sources of beliefs is that the distinction between these sources is not clear-cut. The fact that the work is done as a team where auditors share their views might limit the validity of studying the effect of each of the sources of beliefs on its own. The results of previous studies like that by Bedard and Biggs (1991) which concluded that auditors are fully committed to generated beliefs might not hold true in real situations. Bedard and Biggs themselves admitted that one of the limitations of their study was that consultation with other members of the audit team was not allowed, which does not reflect the practice. Practically, it might not be possible to differentiate between generated and inherited beliefs as these beliefs come out as a result of discussions between members of the audit team.

Belief Frame

Beliefs could be put in one of two frames; the error frame or the environmental frame (McMillan and White, 1993). Precisely, belief frames are a choice in case of analytical review where auditors might find material changes in the financial statements and where they have to attribute these changes either to the existence of errors or to environmental changes.

The interviews' results were not consistent as to whether auditors prefer an error frame or an environmental one. It has been stated that:

> We always start assuming an error and then we have to go back and find out the actual cause for the change. It is safer to assume that there is an error although we hope there isn't (3: 22).
>
> ...It is normally as a result of finding more information. We have to wait and see. But if there are material changes I normally assume there is an error rather than changes in the environment (4: 26).

On the other hand, it has also been indicated if there were material changes in the accounts, they would normally be attributed to changes in the environment. The reason for this view is that most of the sort of clients that large accounting firms deal with would usually have reasonably good accounting systems and records.

> I would normally say changes in the environment. I would say it resulted from business circumstances or the economy or so forth because most of the sort of clients that we have would usually have reasonably good accounting systems and records and

therefore it is unlikely that they present something to you which has an error. Therefore you normally assume that reasons of changes in those numbers are because that is actually affected by their circumstances (5: 22).

However, there were other opinions indicating that auditors do not form beliefs or assumptions about the causes of material changes in the financial statements. Instead auditors have to investigate why the figure is wrong. This is evidenced from the following quotes:

> ...essentially you always expect change and you just have to find out the reason for that change. You don't normally assume the cause for the change (1: 25).
> ...If we find that there is something different we don't form an assumption. One always has to go back to find out the reason (2: 33).
>
> I don't assume anything. I have to go back and find out the causes. I wouldn't say right from the beginning that there is an error. I have to find out the causes (6: 26).
>
> You would never assume anything until you've [addressed] the question with the client. You can't assume because you couldn't know what have caused until somebody's given you an explanation. Unless the client has already told you about something which is then supported by looking at the numbers, but you never make your own assumption about reasons for change without asking and finding out from someone who knows (7: 38).

It was also indicated that analytical review procedures conducted at the end of the audit should normally bring in expected results.

> Well we would, by the time you go to doing the year-end, you know at the end, we would like to think that the analytical review will bring in expected results because we would like to think that we've understood what has gone on that. If there's a variance of what we'd expect the outcome to be, we would be able to explain it because we will have understood what has happened (10: 64).

If there are unexpected fluctuations, auditors would ask the client for an acceptable explanation. If the explanation is unacceptable, auditors would then start assuming that there is an error.

> So I think the, if an analytical review brought on something which is unexpected as you're saying, we'll be assuming that's an error. Again, we would soon get suspicious, we would just investigate and then try and understand it. You know we would look in front of that and say this is what we would, you know why it would happen, you know why this is this from what we expected to be that, and we would get an explanation, and if the client was unable to give us a satisfactory explanation, we would then start going on the route that there's an error there. But we would, you know we would not just automatically jump to that conclusion (10: 64).

On the other hand, the interviews' results showed that beside the error frame and the environmental frame, there is another frame that auditors might choose to put their beliefs in. It has been indicated that if analytical review procedures indicated the existence of material changes in the financial statements, the first assumption that would come to the auditors' minds is that they have missed something in their initial evaluation rather than there being an error, especially in the case of large accounting firms auditing well controlled large companies. This is evidenced from the following quote:

> ... first thing that come to my mind is well I know why there is a material change, what have I missed in my initial evaluation. You know, I think I would, in a controlled large company, I would probably be expecting to understand material changes and I would perhaps assume, initially I would assume that I overlooked something rather than there being an error in particular ... Major sort of Plc's with sophisticated environments, I would assume that I was missing a bit of that sophistication probably (12: 93, 95).

The view that auditors do not assume likely causes of unexpected fluctuations when conducting analytical procedures is the strongest view of the interviewees. However, this view is not consistent with the previous literature. There are many indications in the previous studies that auditors identify likely causes of unexpected fluctuations in the financial statements and that this identification would affect the efficiency and effectiveness of the audit process.

In conducting analytical procedures, auditors tend to generate frequently occurring financial statement errors as their initial beliefs to explain unexpected fluctuations (Heiman-Hoffman et al., 1995). Belief formation in the form of identifying likely causes of unexpected fluctuations is critical to successful performance of a diagnostic task such as analytical procedures (Krishnamoorthy et al., 1997). Koonce (1993) indicated that likely causes of unexpected fluctuations could be self-generated or acquired from other audit team members, working papers or client management.

Church and Schneider (1993, p. 334) argue that in performing analytical procedures, the efficiency and effectiveness of auditors' evidence search are affected by the formation of initial beliefs that identifies likely causes of unexpected fluctuations. They state that:

> Auditors' abilities to accumulate evidence efficiently and effectively may be affected by the way that they formulate diagnostic hypotheses.

Bedard and Biggs (1991) also confirm the previous view that forming beliefs in conducting analytical procedures affects the efficiency and effectiveness of the audit process as evidenced from the following quote (Bedard and Biggs, 1991, p. 622):

Audit efficiency and effectiveness depend on competency in recognizing patterns in financial data and in hypothesizing likely causes of those patterns to serve as a guide for further testing.

Despite all the previous indications in the literature about the formation of beliefs when conducting analytical procedures in the form of likely causes of unexpected fluctuations, the results of the interviews showed that auditors, in most cases, would not act in this way. Practically, auditors would just investigate the reasons for the fluctuations. The results of the interviews are, however, consistent with the UK auditing standard SAS 410.4 which indicates that when unexpected fluctuations are identified, auditors should investigate and obtain adequate explanations and appropriate corroborative evidence.

Expertise

Expertise has been agreed to assist auditors in searching for evidence because experienced auditors have better understanding and can corroborate evidence easily particularly if they have some specialty in the client's industry, and, thus, consume less time and less resources. Less experienced auditors take longer to collect evidence. They also take longer to understand the situation. Consequently, 'if I didn't understand the business and the industry I'm involved with, I need 100% risk assessment' (8: 34). At the same time, 'inexperienced auditors are probably unsure of the significance of the evidence they gather so they will tend to gather lots of evidence, not necessarily appropriate evidence' (11: 101).

Experience would affect the way auditors conduct their work. The more experienced auditor would probably focus his/her work more efficiently because of that experience. It has been pointed out that even though time and cost are quite important and might affect the search for evidence, but it all depends on the experience of the auditor. More experienced auditors are probably better at focusing at what is actually really important, and they are more likely to form plausible assessments.

> Um, I think the basis on which you make those assessments is always that this is preliminary and that it may not be supported by later evidence which comes to light. Having said that, um, an audit manager with sufficient experience and particularly someone who knows a client who we've had for a number of years, you would tend to find that those risk assessments tend to be supported by what we find later on because we know enough about the client to be fairly certain of what we say in the first place, but ... there's certain opportunity to amend those assessments when we do some more detailed work (7: 32).

Although it has been agreed that experience is very important and experienced auditors know what they are doing and what to concentrate on, this does not mean that inexperienced auditors would not be able to perform the work in a good manner because 'less experienced auditors, the staff, they are directed in everything they do. They work within a certain plan and a budgeted time and cost' (6: 30). In addition to this, practically inexperienced auditors are not allocated responsibilities for tasks needing a high level of experience.

> ... we wouldn't do it without people without expertise doing the job ... They're under very very close supervision ... you know I wouldn't get a trainee to go and do something which a senior manager should be doing (10: 79, 81).

Also, the fact that auditors work as a team means that they share their experiences, and it has been stated that:

> ... the older you get, you get a good reaction, if you like, you get a feeling really. I think that the training you have would affect your approach. But as I said we work as a team and we share our experience. So it's very much a team experience (9: 30).

However, less experienced auditors might gather evidence more than needed, but this used to happen more in the past.

Beside experience, the training of the auditors would also affect their approach in searching for evidence together with other factors like knowledge of the business, knowledge of the industry, and intelligence. Expertise itself is a combination of good training and experience in audit practising.

Confirmation Bias

The underlying assumption when talking about confirmation bias is that there is an initial belief and that auditors would try to confirm or deny this belief with the evidence gathered during the audit process. Confirmation bias happens when auditors are committed to their beliefs to the extent that they will try to seek only confirming evidence or assign more weight to confirming evidence. However, the analysis of the interviews revealed that auditors do not feel at all committed to their initial beliefs or opinions. Accordingly, they will not weigh evidence depending on whether it is confirming or disconfirming.

> ... We will gather the evidence with an open mind and then come back and produce the opinion. I don't think there is any point of time while we gather evidence we say that supports and that doesn't. It is not a balance ... The initial opinion is really a basis on which someone can plan but it is not something you are particularly committed to (2: 29, 31).

> When I have an expectation I don't give different weights to evidence depending on whether it supports my expectation or not (4: 34).

The idea of regarding risk assessment as a sort of an initial assumption eliminated the feeling of commitment to this assessment.

... as I say I don't think it is so much a question of forming an opinion. As a fact you're trying to point out yourself to things that you want to find out about. So it is more a sort of identifying areas of risk rather than an opinion and therefore you are looking for evidence to address the concerns that you might have but it is not necessarily evidence which supports or is against a particular opinion. In that sense I haven't got one (5: 18).

I suppose our initial opinion on the risk does not mean that this is what we are going to issue in our report. I mean when you identify risky areas, you say this area is of high risk so we need to focus upon it, and therefore we audit this item carefully. We gather evidence to make us satisfied, but not to confirm or deny, I mean if we find out that the item is OK, this does not deny the fact that it is of high risk ...As I said our initial opinion is risk assessment. If for example we assessed an item as being of high risk, and then we find evidence to tell us that there is something wrong, I do feel that we were right to consider this item to be of high risk. But I think this is different from commitment (6: 22, 24).

I'm quite happy that if I'm wrong then I've learned something ... If I'm identifying something as a risk, I've perceived it to be a risk and then [find it] not to be a risk, I want to know why it's not a risk (8: 24, 26).

If there is evidence to say that you are right to be concerned about a certain area of risk, then that might affect the formation of the final opinion. But it is not commitment.

If there is an area of risk which you are concerned about and there is evidence coming through to say that you are right to be concerned about it, then you might feel that it will affect the formation of the final opinion. But it is not commitment. I feel basically neutral. I mean it doesn't really matter to me what opinion we come to. The fact is that we want to be right (5: 20).

However, if an auditor had assessed something to be of high risk and thereafter there was evidence supporting that fact, the auditor would be negligent not to follow it through to the end. But if there was evidence to change that expectation or assessment, the auditor would have to change it.

I mean you'd hope to confirm it because again in most cases your initial expectation is that, particularly if you're dealing with a client you knew well and he's historically been known by good systems, you'll be hoping to confirm it. Things are again moving to plan because ... you too have a trouble, you have an incentive to remain committed to your initial expectation ... but if you find evidence that suggests things are not the way you expected them to be, you'll be very keen to change it (12: 84).

The classification of evidence to confirming and disconfirming does not have an effect because:

...I don't sit down there and take a huge sigh of relief and say oh that's supports the assumption, that's a good relief. I think depending on the area involved. If it's comparatively low risk straight-forward area then I'm quite happy to have supportive information ...But it's not purely supportive, we then have to weigh supportive against contradictory evidence (8: 38).

Furthermore, one of the interviewees indicated that he does feel committed to his initial opinion. However, this commitment does not mean classifying evidence to confirming and disconfirming.

> Yes probably we are committed to it because as soon as we identify that there is something that we need to look at we have to follow it through to the end. It doesn't mean that we have to end up with the same opinion ... We look for evidence to tell whether we are right or wrong. It doesn't matter which way it goes. All we try to do is to identify facts. But of course as anyone, one would feel happy if his opinion is right (3: 18, 20).

It has also been argued that if there was evidence supporting the initial expectation, this would make auditors feel more committed to it 'I think human nature would probably dictate that yes if you get a body of evidence' (11: 91). However, auditors would still want to wait until the end of the process to evaluate all the evidence gathered 'I think you'll wait for all the testing and then you make up your mind about your initial expectation' (12: 90). Furthermore, one of the interviewees commented that giving more weight to confirming evidence might lead to less objectivity 'I hope we don't give more weight to evidence that supports. One must be objective' (2: 37).

The previous results contradict with the results of other studies (Butt and Campbell, 1989; Ashton and Ashton, 1988 and 1990; and Tubbs et al., 1990) that auditors are more sensitive to disconfirming evidence.

Although there was a strong agreement that auditors in practice do not tend to classify evidence to confirming and disconfirming, it has been indicated that the evidence search strategy in the case of analytical review would very much tend to be a disconfirming one because auditors would be looking for the exceptions. It has been stated that:

> If we were to be doing a text book on good analytical review, we would actually I think ... very much looking to see whether the evidence contradicts our expectations and I think we would again probably be looking for the exceptions rather than accumulating confirmations maybe. I think that we would like to see what's a confirmation but we would have to investigate material exceptions to that hypothesis, couldn't just ignore it (11: 23).

This view is very difficult to be generalised and applied to the entire audit process. It also contradicts with the findings of Ayers and Kaplan (1993) that auditors are prone to confirming strategies during analytical review procedures. However, Ayers and Kaplan's study was based on the underlying assumption that auditors classify evidence to confirming and disconfirming with respect to the initial belief, which might not reflect the reality.

Compliance tests would also be a good example of following a disconfirming search strategy.

> A compliance test would be a good example of actually seeking to disconfirm. You actually are looking for the exception, and I guess the key difference between that is because our compliance test would be sort of statistically based and we would be looking for the exception because if we had an exception potentially, however small, it could actually be very significant (11: 25).

The overwhelming result was that the most significant evidence depends on its source and nature as evidenced from the following quote:

> I don't think you can say that you'd assign more weight to one type of evidence. With the actual nature of the factor that you found in the piece of evidence. I mean there may be one piece of evidence which is very significant which supports, either supports your risk assessment or supports the amount in the financial statements. There may be something which is very minor but doesn't support you, and you have to weigh those things up. Or may be the other way round, you may find something, I suppose, if you find a problem, you would probably find one piece of evidence that suggests that there is a problem with that particular assertion or that particular component, and that may be, it may be so significant, you would have to rethink how much audit, what you need to do, do a lot more work (7: 48).

In addition to this, the way auditors challenge evidence will differ because 'individual's particular approach and personality does vary' (5: 33).

It is, therefore, concluded that the most important evidence is the evidence which comes from a third party and, hence, more weight is assigned to third party written evidence, unless there is 'an incentive with the external party to corrupt things, its reliability might take less' (12: 113).

> It is evidence which comes from a third party. It is not evidence which supports or not, it is evidence which is dependent or independent ... It is the independent evidence which has the greatest effect (1: 29, 33).

> It depends on the source. Third party evidence has more weight whether it is supportive or not (6: 32).

There was a slight disagreement about auditor generated evidence. One of the interviewees indicated that it comes next to third party evidence.

> ...I think it depends on the quality of the evidence. I mean going back to the sort of basic auditing principles that the third party evidence is better than something which you generated yourself which is better than something that is just a representation from the management. So it depends on the source (5: 28).

However, another interviewee commented that auditor generated evidence is the best type of evidence.

I'm still quite keen on the traditional approach which says auditor generated evidence is best, independent evidence is next best, and client provided evidence is least best (8: 40).

It has also been noted that the weight assigned to pieces of evidence differs from case to case. Thus, the most influential type of evidence depends on what the issues and what the risks are. However, independent third party evidence would still be the best type of evidence if it was available.

> if you look at it generically, generically the best type of evidence is independent third party confirmation. But you can't always get independent third party confirmation for everything but there is (10: 83).

The results of the interviews about confirmation bias are quite significant. Previous auditing studies (see for example Butt and Campbell, 1989; Knechel and Messier, 1990, and Ashton and Ashton, 1990) that concluded that auditors are more sensitive to disconfirming evidence based their conclusions on the classification of evidence to confirming and disconfirming with respect to the initial belief. The limitation of previous studies is that in practice this classification might not occur, as indicated by the interviewees, in which case the results of these studies might not be generalisable to actual audit settings.

Professional Scepticism and Conservatism

The results of the interviews indicated that auditors are more cautious than other people. However, generalisation is not appropriate because this would depend to a great extent on the personality of the auditor. But, in general, auditors are more cautious than other people because of their training.

> ...I suspect they are as a breed more cautious. But I don't know whether they're just cautious mattering their work. Sometimes auditors don't seem to be fairly brave about what they do in their non-work tasks...they are just cautious as they used to be as people, but I don't necessarily think their work is any less cautious (8: 44).

So the 'ideal auditor' will always do everything with a healthy dose of scepticism.

> ... I mean it's almost in that training. I think someone might say that the ideal auditor which will always have a healthy, do everything with a healthy dose of scepticism and that is one of the sort of intervenes that a good auditor has, is to be sceptical of management's view. That means they put together, you know, it's something which is the best presentation, and the auditor's job is almost, it might be a little sceptical job (12: 10).

The caution of auditors might have led them in the past to gather evidence more than needed. However, this does not happen these days because of the limited time and cost.

> I think in the past there might have been a tendency to do that. I think these days cost pressures mitigate against that. I think these days there is a sort of tendency that you do the minimum which you feel you would be happy to stand up in the court and say that was enough to support key things ...... [in] the accounts which were relevant to any possible user (5: 35).

Although auditors, in general, are viewed to be more cautious than other people, this caution or conservatism would be reflected mainly in the risk assessment and not directly in auditors' attitudes toward evidence. Auditors are, in particular, more sceptical with new clients.

> I usually have a very very sceptical view of new clients. That's absolutely why I'm searching for evidence to make sure that I'm not taking on risk that I'm not aware of. I guess with existing clients where you had many years of contact, I think perhaps it's slightly less cynical...... [but with new clients] we would have a whole set of risk procedures from the client acceptance which really comes back to my sort of cynical view of a new client. Why has this client wanted to change auditors? Um, you know, have they reasons, disagreements, and we would actually have an extremely cynical process that we go through (11: 9, 19).

Auditors are regarded by the interviewees to be more sceptical and conservative than other people. However, none of their answers supported the previous findings of McMillan and White (1993) that professional scepticism would affect both the initial belief frame and auditors' attitudes toward confirming and disconfirming evidence. It is relevant to point out here that subjects in McMillan and White's study were *asked* to form an initial belief, whereas this might not happen in practice. Although the results of the interviews indicated that auditors might have an initial belief in the form of risk assessment, a clean initial opinion, or even an idea or expectation, the formation of these initial beliefs is not formal and does not receive much attention. In other words, auditors do not sit down and have a belief formulated and put it in a specific frame. '...we don't see that forming an [initial] opinion has got such significance. It's only if we saw it coming up with issues that we thought could have a serious impact' (10: 20).

Diagnostic Content of Evidence

The auditing literature did not provide with a clear insight into the meaning of the term diagnostic content of evidence. While Hackenbrack (1992) referred to diagnostic evidence as relevant evidence and non-diagnostic evidence as irrelevant evidence, McMillan and White (1993) indicated that diagnostic evidence is evidence that allows auditors to distinguish between alternatives, while non-diagnostic evidence does not.

Akresh et al. (1988, p. 52) provided an example of non-diagnostic evidence that is consistent with McMillan and White: '... evidence of zero errors in the sales transaction stream may be consistent with both a proposition that accounts receivable are not overstated and that they are overstated'.

The term 'diagnostic evidence' was not clear to the interviewees, so the previous definitions and example were used to know their attitudes about such type of evidence. The following quotes illustrate the views of the interviewees regarding non-diagnostic evidence.

> ...This is neutral evidence and it will only tend to be in certain areas. This is not evidence. If it is evidence in a critical area we have to go further (2: 41).

> Yes I find evidence like this and I think in this case it will neither support nor deny my opinion so I would have to ignore it (3: 30).

> ...what you intend to do is rather than say I have a piece of evidence here that gives me comfort over sales and may give comfort over debtors, what you would say is right if I'm looking at debtors what evidence do I need to support debtors. What do I need to find to satisfy myself. So I guess you may find pieces of evidence that are compelling and it's supporting one item but not another, but then you would always look for other evidence to support the other one (7: 54).

> ...what we're looking for is the evidence we can actually depend on to give a clean opinion. That's why if we're going to qualify our opinion we've got to have very strong evidence. It's not right that at the end of the day we change our opinion or qualify it without getting further strong evidence (9: 34).

The previous quotes illustrate that the interviewees regarded non-diagnostic evidence to be evidence indicating more than one opinion, in which case they preferred to ignore it as it is not strong evidence. This finding supports the findings of Skov and Sherman (1986) about the predominance of diagnosing search strategies in the area of information gathering.

Evidence Order

Three main views about the effect of evidence order to auditors' decision-making were expressed in the interviews. The first view was that the last piece of evidence is the most important piece.

> I would say the last piece. Imagine bits of evidence coming along all the time. You will always get more from the latest piece of evidence. It is the last piece of evidence that we accept and that will make you ignore the other pieces of evidence. So again the last piece of evidence is the most crucial (1: 43).

> I suspect the latest piece of evidence is more important because after it you stop looking for more evidence. So it is the piece which makes you satisfied (6: 42).

This view is consistent with the findings of previous studies (see for example Asare, 1992; Pei et al., 1992; and Messier and Tubbs, 1994) about the presence of recency effects which means that auditors are more likely to give more weight to the last piece of evidence. However, it has been argued, by the interviewees, that although order is important, it is not the issue of first or last that would affect.

> I don't think it makes any difference ultimately because it's not whether it's first or it's last. It's the quality of the evidence itself which is important (5: 39).

The second view was that order is important if pieces of evidence differ in their strength. Specifically, it would be better if the strong pieces of evidence come first. It has been stated that:

> Well, strong then weak will affect. If you get the strong piece first then you could stop looking for further evidence as long as this strong evidence satisfies you. But if you get the weak piece first then you will still have to go further (3: 36).

So if auditors get strong evidence first then they might stop collecting other evidence. If they get weak evidence first, they still have to get more evidence. However, if the strong evidence comes later they would, according to the interviewees' opinions, assign more weight to it. The order of evidence might also influence auditors' decisions in the case of mixed or contradictory evidence.

> the order and way that you presented things can colour your approach and opinion and clearly if you have contradictory evidence, the order in which you receive it will at any one point in time influence the opinion (5: 37).

The strongest view was that order of evidence is not important and would not affect the auditor's opinion, as illustrated from the following quotes:

> I don't think the order does matter. I mean you would probably ask for them in the order of importance. I mean you would look, you would attempt to find the most important thing first. Very often what we find is that things don't arrive in that order. The person you are asking can't deliver it. You've written to ask for confirmations to a supplier or to a third party and it doesn't arrive. So in the end it's what you've assembled (7: 64).

> I don't think it's the order, because the fact is that at the end of the day you actually look at the evidence you got. You don't ask yourself what is the order in which I received these pieces of evidence. So I don't see any difference because of the order (9: 38).

> ... I don't think the order of getting the evidence is really a factor because it's not as if we are been given the evidence in different sort of, you know, particular order. I think what you better remember is that a lot of the stuff, a lot of the audit that we're doing is not us going searching for evidence, is us asking the client to give us the evidence (10: 94).

This result is consistent with part of the findings of Messier (1992) who supported the existence of recency effects, but concluded that it did not result in different audit reports. To the contrary, Asare (1992) found that recency affected auditors' reports.

Order has also been regarded, by the interviewees, to be unimportant because the amount of evidence is predetermined.

> My feeling, my initial reaction to this question was that you tend to set up-front the amount of evidence that you want to collect and so the order doesn't really matter. But I'm thinking of a test, you might test a sample of ten items, as whatever you do you're going to test ten, and whether the first one confirms or disconfirms it doesn't really matter because you're going to do ten anyway and you're going to look at those out of the ten. I think it again depends on exactly the test that you're doing (12: 119).

Furthermore, it has been argued that what is important is the order of the investigations and not the order of evidence.

> I think it's, I think what is important is, order isn't strictly evidence but is, I think, it is the order in which you've had to conduct your investigations, that I think you have to be perhaps a little bit top-down (11: 118).

Evaluation Mode

Evidence is evaluated either in a SbS mode or an EoS one. The results of the interviews revealed that auditors could employ a SbS mode, an EoS mode, or both modes together. When a SbS mode is employed, pieces of evidence are evaluated sequentially as soon as each piece is received. In some cases the SbS evaluation is employed on a daily basis. In other words, auditors would evaluate pieces of evidence they received each day because 'at the end of the day you would sit down and evaluate what you've got. And the audit progresses this way' (9: 40).

It has also been claimed that a SbS mode would be beneficial especially in case of compliance tests and when negative evidence is evaluated first.

> ... if you're hoping to rely on a controlled system, minimise your detailed work, and the first five compliance tests of the control indicate the controls are not working, you will know you were planning to do ten, you would stop and say look I can't rely on this control. The first five pieces of evidence say it doesn't exist. Forget about the control and do another more detailed substantive testing ... I think the problem is if you're doing different types of tests, if you come back to my control compliance test, if you found the first five pieces of evidence to show the control isn't working, you won't do all ten because you know already the control hasn't worked. So in that case you're tending to look at evidence as you collect it. But on the other hand, for lot of the other work when you're doing substantive tests tend to look at the evidence together when you've done all the tests to see what things are (12: 123, 130).

So in the case of compliance tests auditors tend to look at evidence as they collect it, while in the case of substantive tests, evidence is evaluated in an EoS mode.

With an EoS mode evidence is looked at as a whole for each individual item.

> we would identify an issue and confront it and ask the client to provide us with the evidence. So we probably get it altogether (10: 96).

On the other hand, when both modes are employed, evidence is looked at SbS because it is received sequentially, and at the end auditors try to put it altogether by looking at it globally, in particular by the partner or the manager and this 'can have some advantages in terms of bringing a fresh mind to bear' (8: 50). It has also been indicated that evidence is normally evaluated SbS which is more effective. However, when the audit team, or somebody else, is reviewing the work, evidence is evaluated altogether. So the two different approaches are employed in practice.

However, a different point of view about the evaluation mode employed was that the way of evaluating evidence depends on the client. It has been pointed out that:

> ...some clients are well prepared and are ready to inform you, and what we normally do is request a list of information that we might be [in need of] at the outset of the audit. Some clients do have it and others don't, and the ones that give you everything at the outset make the audit process that much easier...And therefore the way you assess that evidence will obviously be on the basis of what you have at any particular point of time. So our ideal approach would be that if I have everything ready for us, all evidence there, and so forth at the outset so we can consider it in one go. Unfortunately, that is the ideal rather than necessarily the reality (5: 14).

Another different view about the mode employed in evidence evaluation was that the mode employed is dependent on the level of the auditor.

> It really depends on the level. Obviously you have partners, managers, and staff. The staff auditors evaluate evidence sequentially. As soon as they collect a piece of evidence, they evaluate it. Managers look at evidence gathered less frequently, but they don't wait until the end. Partners look at evidence altogether at the end. So it depends very much on the level of the auditor (6: 44).

Finally, it has been indicated that the different ways of evaluating evidence depend on the order in which this evidence is received, and different orders should not lead to differing opinions.

> It shouldn't do. I wouldn't say it couldn't do. I mean it shouldn't do but if you've been objective and sort of keeping up an overview of what you're trying to achieve, your opinion is based on the evidence and it doesn't really matter how that evidence came through to you and in what order. But certainly in the case of clients who want to change their numbers quite a lot during the finalisation process, and they are giving you bits of pieces of new evidence and so forth, then possibly the order in which it came through will have some bearing but hopefully not any (5: 43).

Although previous auditing studies (Ashton and Ashton, 1988; Tubbs et al., 1990; and Trotman and Wright, 1996) investigated the effect of the evaluation mode on auditors' belief revision and the presence of recency effects, none of these studies addressed the issue of whether different evaluation modes would lead to different audit reports. This issue is of great importance as it would directly affect the effectiveness of the audit process.

Time and Cost

The interviewees were asked about their opinions regarding the effect of time and cost on their search for evidence. Their answers indicated that the audit is conducted within a certain budget and timetable. Consequently, time and cost are unlikely to affect auditors' search for evidence. The following quotes illustrate this view:

> ... timetable is very important and when planning the work it is planned according to a timetable and it's very unlikely that you consume or require more than the planned time (1: 37).

> No time and cost are functions of the planning process. The audit is planned through a budget but the opinion is not planned to a budget. So we don't stop if we did not collect enough evidence (2: 45).

> Time because you are working according to a timetable. Cost also can be a problem. But I think these days everything is planned and it is very rare that you face the problem of running out of time or exceeding budget ... Again it is a matter of balance and we've got to be satisfied before giving our opinion (3: 32, 34).

> ... When we plan our work we have a budget and a timetable, and it very unlikely that we find we need to incur more costs and spend more time. So we have our schedules, so time and cost are not points to worry about (9: 36).

It has also been indicated that time and cost are not factors that would affect auditors' search for evidence because if they need to spend more time and incur more costs, they have to do so.

> ... time and cost is something that we do look at carefully, but in the end if you believe that you need to obtain more evidence then you would have to spend the time and incur the cost whether you like it or not. So I don't think that would impact on the work that you do (7: 58).

It should, however, be noted that the previous views about time and cost do not mean that auditors are not looking for the most efficient way of doing the audit. The point is that time and cost should not affect the final opinion. In other words, time and cost are factors of the efficiency and not the effectiveness of the audit. This is evidenced from the following quotes:

Well clearly all auditors and ourselves included, we're in this because it's business. We want to make profit, make money, therefore time and cost are quite relevant. And because a lot of clients are very cost sensitive these days and therefore they are putting you on the pressure to keep your work to an absolute minimum. This affects the search for evidence because given a limited time and resources you could get to the bottom of every last penny in the cash, but the point is that shouldn't be necessarily and the more experienced you are probably the better you are at focusing at what is actually really important. The danger of course is that you go too far the other way and this means that you don't obtain enough information or you can't do the work with sufficient quality or effectively. You're relying on other normal audit work to subsidise the audit work and I think it's a real danger. I mean cost and time are relevant (5: 32).

... the reality is that you haven't got an unlimited budget in doing audit work and you got to work within budgets and fees in order to stay in business and so on ... So cost/effectiveness is the most important thing, but if we identify something as being of high risk ... we would either, we would do it and either negotiate a higher fee or not act for the client. So it's cost/effectiveness really (10: 90).

... I hope we try to do it in few days. You know there's what's the most efficient way of gathering evidence ... in the design of our tests we might look to test an account in one way because it actually does minimise time of disruption of the client staff or whatever else. So might choose a strategy which is more appropriate (11: 115).

... is the evidence from liable, is it cost/effective, you know is that the most efficient way of doing the job, and you look sometimes to get reliability, you have to spend time, and that in that best case you can get reliable evidence quickly and that's, it's the ideal situation to get the audit done and you're happy that you've based your conclusions on reliable evidence (12: 116).

From the previous views, it could, therefore, be concluded that auditors would be looking for the most efficient way of conducting an audit without decreasing its effectiveness. This highlights the importance of investigating the effect of employing the belief revision approach on the efficiency and effectiveness of the audit. If the belief revision approach proved to be of benefit to the audit process, this might have an important implication on the audit practice.

Conclusions

This chapter presented the results of the interviews with respect to the factors affecting auditors evaluation of evidence. The factors discussed with the interviewees are those previously mentioned in the auditing literature about the belief revision approach and the belief-adjustment model.
The analysis of the factors was classified into eight sections; belief formation, expertise, confirmation bias, professional scepticism and conservatism, diagnostic content of evidence, evidence order, evaluation mode, and time and cost.

The discussion of belief formation focused on three issues; the concept of the initial belief, its source, and its frame. With respect to the concept of the initial belief, the interviews' results pointed to two main concepts. The first concept is regarding the risk assessment as an initial belief. This view was a very strong one among the interviewees. However, the idea of having risk assessment as an initial belief did not have an effect of the classification of evidence to confirming and disconfirming, and the interviewees still approached evidence with an open mind. This is attributed mainly to the fact that risk assessment is not something to be revised or updated. Rather, if an area is assessed to be of high risk, it will always be of high risk. The second view of the initial belief was that it would be a clean initial opinion. This view came out from the fact that the sort of clients dealing with large accounting firms are unlikely to produce incorrect statements. This view is also more likely to fit with the belief revision approach as the clean initial opinion is something that can be revised or updated.

The interviewees regarded experience as a factor aiding the search for evidence efficiently. Inexperienced auditors might not be as efficient as experienced auditors. However, the work is done as a team where experience is shared by every member of the team and the work of inexperienced auditors is directed.

Confirmation bias proved to be an issue where contradictions with the previous literature occurred. The results of the interviews pointed out that auditors, even if they form initial beliefs, are not committed to these beliefs. Consequently, evidence is not classified from the point of view that it confirms or disconfirms the initial belief. Evidence, whether confirming or disconfirming, is assigned weight depending on its nature and source. Again, the results of previous studies that auditors are more prone to disconfirming evidence, and in cases to confirming evidence, are based on the underlying assumption that there is a formation of initial beliefs in the form of likelihood assessments of the financial statements' assertions or expected causes of fluctuations.

Although the results of the interviews indicated that auditors might be more sceptical and conservative than other people, especially with new clients, the interviewees did not point out that this would affect their attitudes toward confirming and disconfirming evidence. Rather, it might affect the collection of more evidence than needed. However, this used to happen in the past but not in these days because of the limited time and cost.

The meaning of diagnostic content of evidence was not very clear to the interviewees. When asked about non-diagnostic evidence as evidence not allowing auditors to differentiate between alternatives, most of the interviewees preferred to ignore this type of evidence as it is not strong evidence. Furthermore, it has not been regarded as evidence at all.

Three views about evidence order were expressed. First, that the last piece of evidence is the most important piece which is consistent with previous findings about the existence of recency effects. The second view was that order is important if strong evidence comes first as this will terminate the search for other evidence and, hence, improve the efficiency of the audit. However, the strongest view was that order of evidence is not important and should not affect auditors' decisions. This latter view supports the findings of Messier (1992) but at the same time contradicts the findings of Asare (1992). As the effect of order on auditors' decisions is directly related to the effectiveness of the audit process, it is of great important to consider this issue further.

The results of the interviews indicated that both evidence evaluation modes, SbS and EoS, are employed. Practically, a combination of the two modes is employed as evidence is first evaluated sequentially and then looked at altogether. The interviewees also commented that the evaluation mode might depend on the level of the auditor and it might also depend on whether the client is ready to provide the information requested from the outset or not.

The interviewees also indicated that time and cost should not affect evidence search. However, auditors would always be looking for the most efficient way of conducting the audit without affecting the outcomes.

Although the results of the interviews do not support some of the findings of previous auditing studies, this difference could be attributed mainly to the underlying assumption of the previous studies that auditors follow the belief revision approach where an initial belief is formed and evidence is classified to confirming and disconfirming with respect to this belief. However, the results of the interviews revealed that this might not be the reality. Following this conclusion, it now becomes necessary to investigate the effect of employing the belief revision approach on the audit process as compared to the open mind approach referred to by the interviewees.

Chapter 7

Results of Experiment

Introduction

The aim of this chapter is to present the results of the experiment designed to investigate the differences between the belief revision and open mind approaches.
The following points are addressed in this chapter:
- Basis of comparisons.
- Demographic information about participants.
- Method of analysis.
- Differences between the open mind and belief revision approaches.
- Differences between evidence evaluation modes.
- Comparing risk assessment and the initial belief.

Basis of Comparisons

The experiment aimed mainly at addressing the following research question:
- Are there any benefits from following a belief revision approach in auditing particularly benefits related to improving the efficiency and effectiveness of the audit process?

Beside this main objective, the experiment aimed also at addressing the following questions:
- Does the change in the evidence evaluation mode affect auditors' decisions?
- Are there any differences between risk assessment and the initial belief?

To answer the previous research questions the experiment was designed to include two independent variables; the evidence evaluation approach and the evaluation mode. Two evidence evaluation approaches were manipulated; the open mind approach and the belief revision one. Two evidence evaluation modes were also manipulated; the step-by-step (SbS) mode and the end-of-sequence (EoS) one. This resulted in four experimental groups as shown in table 7.1. These groups are the open mind step-by-step group (O-SbS), the open mind end-of-sequence group (O-EoS), the belief revision step-by-step group (B-SbS), and the belief revision end-of-sequence group (B-EoS).

Table 7.1 The experimental groups

	Mode	
	Open Mind	Belief Revision
Approach		
Step-by-Step	O-SbS	B-SbS
End-of-Sequence	O-EoS	B-EoS

The experimental task was to audit the debtors to check whether they are materially correct. Comparisons are carried between two groups at a time. Comparing the results between the open mind approach and the belief revision is first carried out in the SbS mode between the O-SbS and B-SbS groups, and then in the EoS mode between the O-EoS and B-EoS groups.

The comparisons carried out between the open mind and belief revision groups would provide an answer related to the effect of the belief revision approach on audit efficiency. In order to explore the effect of the approach on audit effectiveness, a 'benchmark opinion' was obtained from a group of partners from one of the then 'Big 6' accounting firms. This opinion was used as a basis to compare between the outcome of the experimental task in case of following an open mind approach and in case of following a belief revision one.

Investigating the effect of the evidence evaluation mode is carried out first in the case of following an open mind approach between the O-SbS and O-EoS groups, and then in the case of following a belief revision approach between the B-SbS and B-EoS groups.

Comparing between risk assessment and the initial belief is carried out in the two belief revision groups; B-SbS and B-EoS.

Demographic Information About Participants

As previously indicated in chapter 4, 154 experiments were sent out and 64 completed ones were received. Thus, the response rate is 41.56%. Table 7.2 shows the position of the respondents and the mean experience for each position. Although the aim was to carry out the experiment with auditors in the same level or position, this was not possible. The initial agreement was to carry out the experiment with year three student trainees and junior auditors because of the time limit for auditors in higher levels. However, because of the low response rate, more experiments had to be sent out to the contact persons in the accounting firms. The contact persons, in their turn, forwarded the experiments to auditors willing to participate regardless of their level.

Table 7.2 Years of experience of participants in the experiment

Position	No.	%	Mean	Std dev	Min	Max
S3/Junior	19	29.7	2.25	0.51	1.17	3.33
Senior/Supervisor	23	35.9	3.65	0.92	2.33	6.60
Senior manager	4	6.3	8.94	2.38	7.50	12.50
Partner	3	4.7	21.92	3.32	20.00	25.75
Missing	15	23.4				

Overall, 19 responses were received from year three student trainees (S3) and juniors with mean experience 2.25 years, 23 responses from seniors and supervisors with mean experience 3.65 years, four responses from senior managers with mean experience 8.94 years, and three responses from partners with mean experience 21.92 years.

The majority of the participants were either trainees and juniors, or seniors and supervisors. There was minor participation from senior managers and partners. This condition created a problem in comparing the position of participants when conducting the analysis. This problem was overcome by grouping both the senior managers and partners with the seniors and supervisors in one group referred to as auditors in higher levels. The result is having two positions; year three student trainees/juniors, and auditors in higher levels.

Method of Analysis

Non-parametric tests were chosen as the method of analysis because of their validity under less restrictive assumptions than parametric tests (Gibbons, 1993). It has also been indicated (Gibbons, 1993) that a non-parametric test should be used when any of the following is true:
1. The data are counts or frequencies of different types of outcomes.
2. The data are measured on a nominal or an ordinal scale.
3. The assumptions required for the validity of the corresponding parametric procedure are not met or cannot be verified.
4. The shape of the distribution from which the sample is drawn is unknown.
5. The sample size is small.
6. The measurements are imprecise.
7. There are outliers and/or extreme values in the data, making the median more representative than the mean.

Three of the conditions listed above are true in this study. First, the shape of the distribution from which the sample is drawn is unknown. Second, the sample size is small especially regarding the number of responses in each single group. Third, the assumptions required for the validity of the parametric tests cannot be verified. These assumptions are that the variables are measured with an equal interval or ratio scale, and the samples are drawn from populations whose variances are equal or homogeneous and whose distributions are normal (Cramer, 1994). With respect to the equal variances and normal distribution, violation of these two assumptions had little effect on the values of parametric tests. However, one exception to this was where both the size of the samples and the variances were unequal. In this case, it is necessary to transform the scores to normality or use a non-parametric test (Cramer, 1994). Thus, the obvious difference in the number of responses between the four groups of the experiment supports the use of non-parametric tests.[1]

The tests are conducted between two groups at a time. The Chi-square test was used to test for differences in categorical (nominal or frequency) variables, while the Mann-Whitney U test was used to test for differences in non-categorical variables.[2] The categorical variables included those with answers yes or no like questions about forming the initial or final opinion and whether there is additional work required or not, and those with rankings like position and degree of participants. The non-categorical variables included those involving the experiment and additional times, and questions that were answered by a percentage.

Differences Between the Open Mind and Belief Revision Approaches

Each of the open mind and belief revision groups is divided into two sub-groups according to the evidence evaluation mode. The comparisons are carried out between the open mind and belief revision groups in the SbS mode (O-SbS and B-SbS), and between the open mind and belief revision groups in the EoS mode (O-EoS and B-EoS). This allows for the differences to be attributed to the approach itself and not the evidence evaluation mode.

Previous studies indicated that following a belief revision approach could improve the efficiency and effectiveness of the audit process (see for example Hogarth and Einhorn, 1992; Church and Schneider, 1993; and Bedard and Biggs, 1991). However, there was no empirical support for this assumption. Previous auditing studies employed the belief revision approach as the assumed approach in evidence evaluation without investigating its applicability in audit settings and its benefits to the audit process.

This study presents an attempt to investigate the effect of employing a belief revision approach on the efficiency and effectiveness of the audit process. This investigation is carried out by comparing the belief revision approach with the open mind approach which the interviewees indicated that they follow in audit practice.

---

[1] The data have also been analysed by parametric tests. Most of the results were almost the same. However, the major differences were in the results of comparing the experiment time in groups O-SbS and B-SbS, comparing the experience of participants in groups B-SbS and B-EoS, and comparing the initial belief in groups B-SbS and B-EoS. Also, some comparisons did not give a result due to the small sample size. This supported the use of non-parametric tests.

[2] Differences will be considered significant at confidence level of 90% or more ($p \leq .1000$).

Efficiency is a relation between inputs and outputs. Glynn (1985, p. 29) defined efficiency as follows:

> Seeking to ensure that the maximum output is obtained from the resources devoted to a department (or programme), or alternatively, ensuring that only the minimum level resources are devoted to a given level of output.

Thus, efficiency of the audit process is about whether an existing procedure can be done in a more cost-effective manner (Higson, 1997, p. 206).

Effectiveness, on the other hand, could be defined as 'Ensuring that the output from any given activity is achieving the desired results' (Glynn, 1985, p. 30). In an audit context, effectiveness is 'an assessment of whether the auditor's approach is achieving its objective' (Higson, 1997, p. 206).

In the current experimental study, time was taken as the determinant of the efficiency. Two different times were taken into account. First, the time consumed by each participant to complete the experiment. Second, the additional time anticipated by each participant in order to complete the additional work needed, if any.

The comparisons between the open mind and belief revision approaches will also involve comparing the number of participants who were able to arrive at a final opinion, and the nature of the final opinion.

The measurement of effectiveness will depend on comparing the results of the experiment with the 'benchmark opinion' provided by a group of partners.

The demographic information requested from the participants was concerned with their experience, position in the firm, and degree subject(s). Experience is measured in terms of years of auditing experience. Participants are classified according to their positions into two groups; trainees/juniors and higher levels. Participants are also classified according to their degrees into two groups; business/economics and other degrees.

The analysis indicates that there are no significant experience, position or degree differences between participants in the O-SbS group and those in the B-SbS group. There is also no significant difference between the position of the participants in the O-EoS and B-EoS groups. However, there are significant differences between the participants in the O-EoS and B-EoS groups regarding their experience ($p = .0862$) and degree ($p = .06717$). Participants in the O-EoS group were more experienced and had more business background than those in the B-EoS group.

The differences in the experience and degree of participants between the O-EoS and B-EoS groups might have an implication on the results of the experiment. Any differences might be attributed to the difference between the participants.

Difference in the Experiment Time

Participants were asked to indicate their starting time after reading the background information, and their ending time after the last question about the expected additional time. The difference between the two times was calculated to represent the experiment time each participant spent to complete the task.

Table 7.3 shows that in the O-SbS group, the mean experiment time was 34 minutes, while in the B-SbS group the mean time was 24.857 minutes. This means that each participant in the O-SbS group took, on average, about nine minutes more to complete the experiment than a participant in the B-SbS group.

Table 7.3 Mean experiment time, additional time, and final opinion

	Mean	Std dev	Median	Min.	Max.
1. Experiment time (in minutes)					
O-SbS	34.000	9.760	30.000	15.000	46.000
B-SbS	24.857	10.257	25.000	10.000	45.000
O-EoS	31.897	9.432	30.000	15.000	50.000
B-EoS	27.333	4.716	25.500	20.000	35.000
2. Additional time (in hours)					
O-SbS	3.938	2.821	3.000	0.500	7.500
B-SbS	4.659	3.536	4.000	1.500	14.000
O-EoS	9.021	12.502	6.500	1.000	64.000
B-EoS	4.917	2.976	4.250	1.500	10.000
3. Final opinion %					
O-SbS	.900	-	-	.900	.900
B-SbS	.843	.089	.850	.700	.950
O-EoS	.811	.074	.800	.700	.900
B-EoS	.767	.153	.800	.600	.900

The results of the Mann-Whitney U test shown in table 7.4 indicate that there is a significant difference ($p = .0262$) in the time of completing the experiment between participants in the O-SbS group and those in the B-SbS group. The mean rank in the O-SbS group is 15.89 while in the B-SbS group is 9.50. This means that participants in the belief revision group took significantly less time to complete the experiment than those in the open mind group.

Table 7.3 shows that the mean experiment time of the O-EoS group is 31.897 minutes while that of the B-EoS group is 27.333 minutes. This means that participants in the O-EoS group spent more time to complete the experiment than those in the B-EoS group. The difference is about five minutes. Table 7.4 shows that there is a significant difference between the two groups in the time of completing the experiment ($p = .0849$). The mean rank of the experiment time is higher in the O-EoS group than in the B-EoS one. This means that participants in the B-EoS group took significantly less time to complete the experiment.

If the previous result is linked with the result of comparing the demographic information of the participants in the two groups (O-EoS and B-EoS), the difference in the experiment time might be attributed to the difference in the experience and degree of the participants and not only to the difference in the approach.

Table 7.4 Mann-Whitney U test in comparing the belief revision and open mind approaches

	Experiment time	Additional time	Final opinion %
1. O-SbS & B-SbS			
Mean rank			
O-SbS	15.89	9.25	6.00
B-SbS	9.50	10.55	4.29
U stat	28.0	38.0	2.0
Z stat	-2.2230	-0.4987	-0.6667
P-value	.0262	.6180	.5050
2. O-EoS & B-EoS			
Mean rank			
O-EoS	23.05	19.96	6.72
B-EoS	16.04	15.58	5.83
U stat	114.5	109.0	11.5
Z stat	-1.7227	-1.1792	-0.3806
P-value	.0849	.2383	.7035

Comparing the demographic information of participants in the O-EoS and B-EoS groups showed that participants in the O-EoS group are more experienced than those in the B-EoS group. Besides, there are more participants in the O-EoS group with a degree in business. This means that the more experienced group with the more business background (O-EoS group) took more time in completing the experiment. As efficiency is expected to increase and not decrease with experience and business background, the significant difference in the experiment time between the O-EoS and B-EoS groups could be attributed to the difference between the open mind and belief revision approaches.

Difference in the Expected Additional Time

In the both the O-SbS and the B-SbS groups most participants indicated that that additional work was needed (89% of particpants iin the O-SbS group and 86% in the B-SbS group). The results of the Chi-square test shown in table 7.5 indicate that the difference between the two groups is not significant (p = .82538) Table 7.3 shows that the mean expected additional time in the O-SbS group was 3.94 hours, while that in the B-SbS group was 4.66 hours. This means that participants in the B-SbS group anticipated more additional time than those in the O-SbS group. However, the results of the Mann-Whitney U test in table 7.4 show that there is no significant difference between the expected additional time indicated by the participants in the two groups (p = .6180).

Table 7.5 Chi-square test in comparing the belief revision and open mind approaches

	No. of participants	
	Need additional work	Able to form final opinion
1. O-SbS & B-SbS		
Pearson Chi-square	0.04868	3.65231
DF	1	1
P-value	.82538	.05599
2. O-EoS & B-EoS		
Pearson Chi-square	2.35632	0.35248
DF	1	1
P-value	.12478	.55271

In the EoS mode most participants indicated also that that additional work was needed (83% of particpants iin the O-EoS group and 100% in the B-EoS group). The results of the Chi-square test shown in table 7.5 indicate that the difference between the two groups is not significant (p = .12478) Table 7.3 shows the mean expected additional time for both the O-EoS and B-EoS groups. Participants in the O-EoS group who said that additional work is needed anticipated that, on average, 9.02 hours is needed to complete this work. In the B-EoS group, participants expected to spend, on average, 4.92 hours to do the additional work. However, this difference between the two groups existed as a result of only one participant in the O-EoS group indicating that an extra 64 hours is needed to do the additional work. The results shown in table 7.4 indicate that there is no significant difference between the O-EoS and B-EoS groups regarding the expected additional time (p = .2383).

Difference in the Final Opinion

The results indicate that in the O-SbS group 11% of the participants were able to give a final opinion. In the B-SbS group 50% of the participants were able to give their final opinion. The results shown in table 7.5 indicate that the difference between the two groups is significant (p = .05599). More participants were able to give their final opinion in the belief revision group although both groups were provided with the same background information and same pieces of evidence presented in the same SbS mode.

In the O-SbS group the mean final opinion is that debtors are likely to be materially correct by 90%. In the B-SbS group, the mean is 84.3%. The results of the Mann-Whitney U test in table 7.4 show that with regards to those who were able to give their final opinion in the two groups, the difference in the nature of their opinions is not significant (p = .5050).

Thus, it could be concluded that although more participants in the B-SbS group were able to arrive at a final opinion, no significant difference is found between the B-SbS and O-SbS groups in the nature of the final opinion.

In comparing the final opinion of participants in the O-EoS and B-EoS, the results show that in the O-EoS group 35% of the participants were able to arrive at a final opinion, while in the B-EoS group 25% arrived at an opinion. There is no significant difference between the two groups (p = .55271). The mean final opinion for participants in the O-EoS group is 81.1% (debtors are likely to be materially correct by 81.1%), while that of participants in the B-EoS group is 76.7%. Table 7.4 shows that there is no significant difference between the final opinion % for participants who were able to arrive at it in both the O-EoS and B-EoS groups (p = .7035).

Comparison with the Benchmark Opinion

Measuring the effectiveness of an audit is not an easy task. Joyce (1976, p. 30) indicated that:

> One of the difficulties involved in studying the validity of auditors' judgments is the absence of a suitable criterion by which to distinguish correct from incorrect judgments. Because strict guidelines for information collection and evaluation do not exist, there are no clear-cut "right" judgments available with which to compare individual professional judgments in most audit work.

In an attempt to find out about the effectiveness of following the belief revision approach, a group of partners from one of the then 'Big 6' accounting firms completed the experimental task and came out with an opinion which was considered as a 'benchmark opinion'. They were given the experiment and asked to complete the page including the final opinion and an estimate of the additional work and time needed, if any.

The group of partners came out with a conclusion that no final opinion about the debtors could be given at this stage and that additional work was needed. Most of the additional work needed involved discussions with the client about issues like the significant increase in the debtors balances, reasons for increasing the debtor collection period, debtors with significant balances, the account balances in excess of credit limits, reasons for references not taken up, and whether a provision is required for sales returns and discounts. Other additional work involved checking whether planned substantive tests took account of the controls tests that failed, reviewing the individual debtors accounts for unusual trends, reviewing the accounts and payment history of customers who did not confirm the circularised balances, checking whether unauthorised sales returns were correctly treated, and checking presentation of debtors in the financial statements and whether related parties, if any, have been properly treated. The budgeted time for the additional work has been estimated to be between 3.5 and 7 hours. However, it has been stated that more time might be required depending on the circumstances.

As effectiveness is measured in terms of achieving the required outcome, comparing the results of the experiment with the 'benchmark opinion' will enable to draw some conclusions about the effect of the belief revision behaviour on the effectiveness of the audit process. In the SbS evidence evaluation mode, it has been found that there is significant difference between the open mind and belief revision groups regarding the number of participants who were able to issue a final opinion. However, no significant difference was found in the nature of the final opinion.

More participants in the B-SbS group were able to arrive at a final opinion than those in the O-SbS group (p = .05599). Surprisingly, 71% of the participants in the B-SbS group who were able to issue a final opinion still said that additional work is needed. One possible explanation for this contradiction is that they were not completely sure of their final opinion. This conclusion is supported by the result in the case of the EoS mode where no significant difference was found between the open mind and belief revision groups (O-EoS and B-EoS) regarding the number of participants who were able to issue a final opinion. Furthermore, 50% of the participants in the O-EoS group who were able to issue a final opinion also indicated that additional work was still needed. This again supports the conclusion that participants in all groups tended to arrive at the same conclusion that a final opinion could not be issued at this stage and that additional work was needed. This is consistent with the 'benchmark opinion'.

With regards to the additional time needed, the mean additional times in three of the experimental groups (O-SbS, B-SbS, and B-EoS) fall within the range indicated in the benchmark opinion (between 3.5 and 7 hours). Only the O-EoS group is an exception. The mean additional time in this group is 9.02 hours. However, this is a result of an extreme estimate of one participant in the O-EoS group who anticipated an additional time needed of 64 hours.[3]

Most participants in the four groups were consistent with what has been stated in the 'benchmark opinion' about the nature of the additional work needed.

Discussion

Comparing the open mind and belief revision approaches in both the SbS and EoS evidence evaluation modes came out with some important results. The analyses indicated that there are significant differences in the time of completing the experiment between the open mind and belief revision groups in both evidence evaluation modes. The significant difference in the experiment time could have important implications on the efficiency of the audit process.

Participants in the B-SbS group spent the least time in completing the experiment (mean time 24.857 minutes), followed by participants in the B-EoS group (mean time 27.333 minutes). Participants in the two open mind groups (O-SbS and O-EoS) spent more time in completing the experiment. In the O-EoS group, the mean time was 31.897 minutes, while in the O-EoS group it was 34

---

[3] The mean expected additional time in the O-EoS group was 6.630 when the extreme value was excluded.

minutes. The importance of this result is that it points toward the possibility of reducing the time needed to complete an audit by following the belief revision approach.

The findings also indicated that there are no significant differences between the groups in the expected additional time. However, the significant difference between the open mind and belief revision groups in the experiment time could be viewed as the stronger result. While the experiment time is the *actual* time spent by each participant to complete the experiment, the additional time is a hypothetical time indicated by the participants and refers to the time they *think* is needed to complete the task.

Time and cost are important factors especially these days when accounting firms are trying to complete more audits in less time because of the increasing work load. This simply means that any approach that could lead to a more efficient audit without affecting its effectiveness would be of great benefit. Consequently, as the belief revision approach proved to be more efficient, it should be considered by auditors in doing their work.

The comparison with the benchmark opinion leads to a conclusion that it is not likely that the belief revision approach would affect the effectiveness of the audit process whether by increasing or decreasing it. In other words, following a belief revision behaviour is not likely to lead to better (or worse) auditors' opinions than when following an open mind approach. The benefits of following the belief revision approach are more likely to be related to the efficiency of the audit process.

Differences Between Evidence Evaluation Modes

Evidence could be evaluated either in a SbS mode or an EoS one. Comparisons between the two evidence evaluation modes are carried out once between the two open mind groups (O-SbS and O-EoS), and once between the two belief revision groups (B-SbS and B-EoS) to allow for any differences to be attributed to the evidence evaluation mode.

Differences Between the SbS and EoS Modes in the Open Mind Approach

To investigate the differences between the SbS and EoS modes in the open mind approach, comparisons are conducted between the O-SbS and O-EoS groups. The comparisons involve investigating the differences between the two groups regarding the experiment time, expected additional time, and final opinion.

There is no significant difference between participants in the O-SbS and O-EoS groups regarding their degree ($p = .87644$), while there are significant differences with regards to their experience ($p = .0682$) and position ($p = .00023$). The mean rank of the experience of the participants in the O-EoS group (19.85) is higher than that in the O-SbS group (12.67). This means that the participants in the O-EoS group are more experienced than those in the O-SbS group. This is supported by the result that significantly more participants in the O-EoS group are in higher levels (seniors/senior managers/partners) than those in the O-SbS group. Thus, any differences in the results of the experiment might be attributed to the difference between the participants themselves and not only to the difference in the evidence evaluation mode.

Table 7.6 Mann-Whitney U test in comparing the evidence evaluation modes

	Experiment time	Additional time	Belief 1	Belief 2	Final opinion%
1. O-SbS & O-EoS Mean rank					
O-SbS	21.22	11.81	-	-	9.00
O-EoS	18.97	18.06	-	-	5.11
U stat	115.0	58.5	-	-	1.0
Z stat	-0.5399	-1.6403	-	-	-1.2572
P-value	.5892	.1009	-	-	.2087
2. B-SbS & B-EoS Mean rank					
B-SbS	11.61	11.50	11.75	14.82	6.00
B-EoS	15.71	12.46	14.59	11.96	4.33
U stat	57.5	60.5	59.5	65.5	7.0
Z stat	-1.3941	-0.3404	-0.9621	-0.9636	-0.8126
P-value	.1633	.7336	.3360	.3352	.4164

Difference in the experiment time between the O-SbS and O-EoS groups The mean experiment time for participants in the O-SbS group is 34 minutes, while that for participants in the O-EoS group is 31.897 minutes. This means that participants in the O-EoS group took slightly less time to complete the experiment than those in the O-SbS group. The results of the Mann-Whitney U test shown in table 7.6 indicate that the difference between the two groups is not significant (p = .5892). Even with the experiences and positions of the participants in the two groups being significantly different, this did not affect the difference in the time of completing the experiment.

This result might be an indication that the time of completing an audit is not likely to be affected whether evidence is evaluated in a SbS mode or an EoS one.

Difference in the expected additional time between the O-SbS and O-EoS groups Table 7.7 shows that there is no significant difference (p = .65951) between the O-SbS and O-EoS groups regarding the number of participants who said that additional work was needed and those who did not. In both groups, most participants indicated that additional work was needed to complete the experimental task.

Table 7.7 Chi-square test in comparing the evidence evaluation modes

	No. of participants	
	Need additional work	Able to form final opinion
1. O-SbS & O-EoS		
Pearson Chi-square	0.19413	1.82409
DF	1	1
P-value	.65951	.17683
2. B-SbS & B-EoS		
Pearson Chi-square	1.85714	1.70625
DF	1	1
P-value	.17295	.19147

Participants in the O-SbS group expected to spend on average 3.938 hours to carry out the additional work needed, while those in the O-EoS group expected to spend on average 9.021 hours. The results of the Mann-Whitney U test shown in table 7.6 indicate that there is a slight significance (p = .1009) in the expected additional time between participants in the O-SbS group and those in the O-EoS one. However, this result should be taken with caution for three reasons. First, the result is significant at a confidence level of 89.91%. Second, the difference between the O-SbS and O-EoS groups might be attributed to the significant differences between the experiences and positions of the participants in the two groups. Third, as previously indicated, one of the participants in the O-EoS group indicated that 64 additional hours was needed to complete the task. This resulted in making the mean expected additional time in the O-EoS group higher than other groups.

Difference in the final opinion between the O-EoS and O-SbS groups With regards to the difference in the final opinion due to the difference in the evidence evaluation mode, in the O-SbS 11% of the participants were able to arrive at a final opinion, while in the O-EoS group 35% were able to give their final opinion. However, the difference between the two groups is not significant (p = .17683).

In the O-SbS group, the mean final opinion for the participants who were able to arrive at it was 90% (debtors are likely to be materially correct by 90%), while that for the participants in the O-EoS group was 81.1%. The results in table 7.6 show that there is no significant difference (p = .2087) between the two groups.

Differences Between the SbS and EoS Modes in the Belief Revision Approach

Comparisons between evidence evaluation modes in case of employing a belief revision approach are carried out between the B-SbS and B-SbS groups. Investigating the differences between the two groups involved conducting the following comparisons:
- Difference in the experiment time.
- Difference in the expected additional work and time.

- Difference in the belief after tests of control (Belief 1).
- Difference in the belief after substantive tests (Belief 2).
- Difference in the final opinion.

There are no significant differences between participants in the B-SbS group and those in the B-EoS one regarding their experience (p = .6789, position (p = .26459), and degree (p = .19172). This means that any difference between the two groups could be attributed to the difference in the evidence evaluation mode.

Difference in the experiment time between the B-SbS and B-EoS groups The mean experiment time was 24.875 minutes for participants in the B-SbS group, and 27.333 minutes for participants in the B-EoS group. This means that participants in the B-SbS group took less time to complete the experiment than those in the B-EoS group. Table 7.6 shows that there is no significant difference (p = .1633) in the experiment time between the two groups. This means that the difference in the evidence evaluation mode had no effect on the time of completing the experiment.

Difference in the expected additional time between the B-SbS and B-EoS groups In the B-SbS group 86% of participants indicated that additional work is needed to complete the task compared to 100% of participants in the B-EoS group. The difference between the two groups is not significant (p = .17295).

The mean expected additional time was 4.66 hours for participants in the B-SbS group, and 4.92 hours for those in the B-EoS group. The results of the Mann-Whitney U test shown in table 7.6 indicate that the difference between the two groups is not significant (p = .7336).

Difference in the belief after tests of control between the B-SbS and B-EoS groups Participants in the B-SbS and B-EoS groups were asked to revise their beliefs or expectations about the likelihood that debtors are materially correct after being presented with pieces of evidence from tests of control. In the B-SbS group participants were asked to revise the belief after each piece of evidence. On the other hand, participants in the B-EoS group were asked to revise the belief once after being presented with all pieces of evidence. The comparison is made between the revised belief or expectation after evaluating the last piece of evidence from tests of controls in the B-SbS group and between the belief after evaluating all pieces of evidence from tests of controls in the B-EoS group. A comparison of the mean revised beliefs after evaluating evidence from tests of controls for participants in both the B-SbS and B-EoS groups is shown in table 7.8. The variable is referred to as belief 1.

Table 7.8 Mean beliefs of participants in the B-SbS and B-EoS groups

Variable	Group	Mean	Std dev	Median	Min.	Max.
Initial belief	B-SbS	.633	.058	.600	.600	.700
	B-EoS	.633	.379	.800	.200	.900
Belief 1	B-SbS	.486	.232	.525	.100	.900
	B-EoS	.574	.188	.600	.250	.850
Belief 2	B-SbS	.800	.104	.800	.600	.950
	B-EoS	.748	.137	.775	.500	.900

The mean belief 1 was that debtors are likely to be materially correct by 48.6% for participants in the B-SbS group, and 57.4% for participants in the B-EoS group. This means that participants who evaluated evidence from tests of control in an EoS mode had higher beliefs than those who evaluated evidence in a SbS mode. However, the results of the Mann-Whitney U test shown in table 7.6 indicate that the difference between the two groups is not significant (p = .3360).

Difference in the belief after substantive tests between the B-SbS and B-EoS groups
The result that the evidence evaluation mode has no effect on auditors' opinions is also supported by comparing belief 2 in the B-SbS and B-EoS groups. Belief 2 refers to the revised belief after evaluating evidence from substantive tests. In the B-SbS group participants were asked to revise the belief after each piece of evidence from substantive tests, while participants in the B-EoS group were asked to revise the belief once after being presented with all pieces of evidence. The comparison is made between the revised belief after evaluating the last piece of evidence from substantive tests in the B-SbS group and between the belief after evaluating all pieces of evidence from substantive tests in the B-EoS group.

Table 7.8 shows that the mean belief 2 was that debtors are likely to be materially correct by 80% for participants in the B-SbS group, and 74.8% for participants in the B-EoS group. This means that, unlike belief 1, participants who evaluated evidence from substantive tests in a SbS mode had higher beliefs than those who evaluated evidence in an EoS mode. The results of the Mann-Whitney U test shown in table 7.6 indicate the difference between the B-SbS and B-EoS groups for belief 2 is not significant (p = .3352).

Difference in the final opinion between the B-SbS and B-EoS groups Comparing the final opinion of participants in the B-SbS and B-EoS groups supports the result that the evidence evaluation mode has no effect on auditors' opinions. In the B-SbS group, 50% of participants were able to arrive at a final opinion compared to 25% the B-EoS group. The difference between the two groups is not significant (p = .19147).

The mean final opinion was that debtors are likely to be materially correct by 84.3% for participants in the B-SbS group, and by 76.7% for participants in the B-EoS groups. This means that participants in the B-SbS group had higher likelihood assessments than those in the B-EoS group. Table 7.6 shows that the difference between the two groups is not significant (p = .4164). This means that participants who were able to give their final opinion arrived at the same conclusion whether they followed a SbS mode or an EoS one.

Discussion

The results of comparing the effect of the evidence evaluation mode on auditors' opinions indicated that there are no significant differences between the SbS and EoS modes whether an open mind approach was employed or a belief revision one. A few auditing studies addressed the effect of the evidence evaluation mode on auditors' belief revisions and on order effects.

Ashton and Ashton (1988) concluded that the evaluation mode affected auditors' belief revisions. They found that auditors revised their beliefs to a greater extent when following a SbS mode than when following an EoS mode. Tubbs et al. (1990) found in one of their experiments the presence of order effects only in the SbS mode. This result was supported by the findings of Trotman and Wright (1996) who concluded that senior managers displayed a marginal recency in the SbS mode only in evaluating the internal controls over the debtors. Although the studies of Ashton and Ashton (1988), Tubbs et al. (1990), and Trotman and Wright (1996) did not go further to investigate whether different evidence evaluation modes would lead to different final opinions, their results imply that there might be an effect. This contradicts the results presented above indicating no significant differences between the SbS and EoS modes.

The results of the current study are based on a more comprehensive comparison between the SbS and EoS modes than the previous studies. Ashton and Ashton (1988), Tubbs et al. (1990) and Trotman and Wright (1996) based their comparisons on the differences between the final and initial likelihood judgements of the subjects.

In the current study, the comparison between the SbS and EoS modes in the open mind approach was based on the differences in the experiment time, expected additional work and time, and final opinion. In the belief revision approach, the comparison was based on the experiment time, expected additional work and time, belief after evaluating evidence from tests of controls, belief after evaluating evidence from substantive tests, and the final opinion.

Although the failure to find a significant difference does not demonstrate that in practice following either a SbS or an EoS mode would not affect auditors' opinions, the results of the experiment are consistent with the results of the interviews discussed in chapter 6. The interviewees stated that the difference in the evaluation modes should not lead to different opinions. This result is important for the audit practice.

It has been indicated by the interviewees, that both evidence evaluation modes are employed in practice as evidence is first evaluated sequentially and then looked at altogether. Furthermore, the evaluation mode is more likely to depend on the level of the auditor. Normally, staff auditors evaluate evidence on a SbS basis, while managers and partners are more likely to evaluate it on an EoS basis. Thus, it is of great importance to ensure that both evidence evaluation modes would lead to the same opinion.

Comparing Risk Assessment and the Initial Belief

Comparing risk assessment and the initial belief is based on the two belief revision groups; B-SbS and B-EoS. In both groups, participants were asked after reading the background information if they could form an initial expectation (i.e., initial belief) about the likelihood that debtors are materially correct. They were asked to put their expectation in the form of a ratio ranging from 0% to 100% where 0% is very unlikely that debtors are materially correct and 100% is very likely. Participants were then asked if they considered this initial expectation, whether they formed it or not, as their risk assessment.

Table 7.9 Chi-square test in comparing the initial belief and risk assessment

	No. of participants	
	Able to form initial belief	Risk is initial belief
Pearson Chi-square	1.000	7.5385
DF	1	1
P-value	.3173	.0060

It should be noted that the questions regarding the formation of the initial belief and risk assessment were not affected by the difference in the evidence evaluation mode between the B-SbS and B-EoS groups because pieces of evidence were not presented at this stage. Thus, the results could be analysed by combining the two groups together.

By looking at the results collectively for both the B-SbS and B-EoS groups, it was found that 40% of participants agreed that risk assessment is the same as the initial belief which is a percentage ranging from 0 to 100 and indicating whether debtors are likely to be materially correct or not. However, 60% of participants in the two groups did not agree that risk assessment would be the same as the initial expectation. The results presented in table 7.9 show that the difference between the number of participants who agreed that risk assessment is the same as the initial belief and those who disagreed is not significant (p = .3173). This means that no specific conclusion could be arrived at regarding the nature of the initial belief and whether it is viewed as risk assessment or not.

The participants who disagreed that the initial belief was their risk assessment gave different answers regarding their risk assessment. Most of the answers indicated that at this stage it would be difficult to assess the risk because of the need for further information. Other answers indicated that risk assessment is put in the form of high, normal, or low and not in the form of an initial expectation about the likelihood that debtors are materially correct. One of the participants indicated that risk assessment = 100 - the initial expectation. This means that if the initial expectation is debtors are likely to be materially correct by 70%, then there is a 30% risk that they are over or under-stated.

It is also worth to consider the ability to form an initial belief after reading the background information. The evaluation mode had no effect at this stage of the experiments, and, hence, both the B-SbS and B-EoS groups were similar in all the independent variables. Thus, the results regarding the formation of the initial belief could be discussed as a whole.

In both the B-SbS and B-EoS groups, only 23% of participants were able to give an initial belief at this early stage. The rest of the participants were unable to give an initial belief because of the insufficient information at this stage. It has been indicated that before being able to form an initial belief more evidence is needed to check that the controls are working adequately. It has also been stated that some substantive testing need to be done before arriving at an initial expectation about the debtors.

To compare between the overall number of participants who were able to form an initial belief and those who were not, the Chi-square test was conducted and the result shown in table 7.9 indicates that there is a significant difference (p = .0060) between the number of participants who formed an initial belief and those who did not. Most participants were not able to form an initial belief after reading the background information. This highlights the difficulty of forming initial beliefs at an early stage of the audit.

The previous results in comparing the initial belief and risk assessment raise two main points. First, the difficulty of forming an initial belief at an early stage of the audit process. This does not, however, mean that the belief revision approach could not be employed in auditing. Auditors could form the initial belief at a later stage during the audit and then start employing the belief revision approach in their subsequent evaluation of evidence. The second point is that the concept of the initial belief is not clear to the auditors. It is obvious that auditors are not willing to form an initial belief without having sufficient evidence and do not accept the fact that it is just an *initial* belief that could be changed after receiving pieces of evidence.

The difficulty of forming an initial belief at an early stage of the audit is clear from the result that 23% of participants in the two belief revision groups were able to form an initial belief or expectation. 67% out of them were able to arrive at a final opinion in the end. This represents 40% of the total number of participants who were able to arrive at a final opinion. Interestingly, the other 60% of participants who were able to arrive at a final opinion were participants who did not form initial beliefs after reading the background information. This consequently means that forming an initial belief from the beginning might not have an effect on the formation of the final opinion. This is supported by comparing the initial belief of the participants who formed it with their final opinion. The comparison showed that for all those participants, their final opinion is different from their initial belief.

An important result also is that the participants who were able to form an initial belief changed or revised this belief after being presented with pieces of evidence from tests of controls. They also changed their revised belief, except one of them, after being presented with pieces of evidence from substantive tests. This comparison between the initial belief and the subsequent revised beliefs leads to a conclusion that auditors, even those who formed an initial belief at an early stage were not committed to it and were willing to change it in light of the evidence received.

The previous results support the findings of the interviews in chapter 6. First, the concept of the initial belief is not well established in the mind of the auditors. While some of them regarded their risk assessment to be the initial belief, others did not accept this view. The results of the experiment showed that there is no significant difference between the two views. Thus, no specific conclusion could be drawn regarding the difference between risk assessment and the initial belief. Second, the formation of an initial belief does not mean ending with the same belief. In fact, auditors are willing to change their beliefs depending on pieces of evidence gathered.

The answers of the participants also provided some insight about the measurement of risk assessment. Most of the participants who provided an assessment of risk, put it in the form of high, medium, or low with no differentiation between the components of risk. This supports the discussion in chapter 6 that auditors in practice do not have a clear distinction between inherent, control, and detection risk. Rather, risk is measured by an overall assessment, which supports the findings of Peters (1990). One of Peters' results, that he described as somewhat surprising, was that auditors did not treat inherent, control, and detection risk independently.

The previous finding about risk assessment is very important as it highlights the gap between the audit practice and literature. While in practice risk assessment is done subjectively as an overall assessment, audit studies, on the other hand, focus on the measurement of risk components quantitatively which are then incorporated in a risk model to come out with the overall assessment of risk.

Conclusions

This chapter presented the results of the experiment carried out mainly to investigate the differences between the belief revision and open mind approaches. The experiment was divided into two main groups; an open mind group and a belief revision one. Each of the two main groups was divided into two sub-groups depending on the evidence evaluation mode. This resulted in having four experimental groups; O-SbS, O-EoS, B-SbS, and B-EoS. 64 completed experiments were received from all four groups. Comparisons between the results of the experiment were carried out between two groups at a time and aimed at finding out the differences between the belief revision and open mind approaches, differences between evidence evaluation modes, and differences between risk assessment and the initial belief. The limitation of the results should be noted due to the relatively small number of participants and the lack of other studies addressing the same issues.

Comparisons between the open mind and belief revision approach were conducted between the two groups in the SbS mode, and between the two groups in the EoS mode. The results showed that following the belief revision approach led to completing the experiment in less time than when following the open mind approach. However, the difference was more significant in the SbS mode. The results also showed that more participants in the B-SbS group were able to arrive at a final opinion, although most of them indicated that additional work is still needed.

The answers of the participants in the open mind and belief revision groups were also compared with a 'benchmark opinion' received from a group of partners from one of the then 'Big 6' firms. The comparison showed that there were no differences between the participants' answers and the 'benchmark opinion'.

The previous results led to the conclusion that following a belief revision approach might affect the efficiency of the audit process. Completing the experiment in less time means that following a belief revision approach could lead to a more efficient audit. This result has some important implications on the audit practice. Auditors in practice might have to consider employing the belief revision approach to increase the efficiency of the audit process especially with the time limit due to the increasing work load in accounting firms.

Another comparison discussed in this chapter was concerned with the evidence evaluation mode. The comparison was first carried out between the SbS and EoS modes in the open mind approach, and then between the two modes in the belief revision approach. No significant differences between the two evidence evaluation modes were found. This result is consistent with the views of the interviewees discussed in chapter 6 that evidence evaluation modes should not affect auditors' opinions. On the other hand, the result is not consistent with previous auditing studies (Ashton and Ashton, 1988; and Tubbs et al., 1990) that found out that the evidence evaluation mode had an effect on auditors' belief revisions and on the recency effects displayed in their decisions. This, consequently, implies that different evidence evaluation modes might lead to different opinions. The contradiction between the results of this study and the results of previous studies supports the need for further investigation of this issue.

The last comparison carried out in this chapter is comparing between the initial belief and risk assessment. The results indicated that some of the participants viewed risk assessment to be the same as the initial belief (a percentage indicating the likelihood that the debtors are materially correct), while others disagreed with this. However, no significant difference was found between the number of participants agreeing and those disagreeing. This led to the conclusion that the concept of the initial belief is not well established which supports the results of the interviews.

It has also been found that most participants were not able to form an initial belief at an early stage of the audit. While only 23% of participants in the two belief revision groups were able to form an initial belief after reading the background information, 96% of them formed a belief after being presented with evidence from tests of controls. Furthermore, comparing the answers of the participants showed that they did not end up with the same initial belief.

Chapter 8

Discussion and Conclusions

Introduction

This study aimed at investigating the effect of the belief revision approach on auditors' evaluation of evidence. This concluding chapter summarises and discusses the findings of the empirical study presented in the previous three chapters.

The following points are addressed in this chapter:
- Findings of the empirical study.
- Implications of the findings of the empirical study.
- Areas for future research.

Findings of the Empirical Study

The empirical study addressed the following research questions:
1. Do auditors in practice follow a belief revision approach in their evaluation of evidence?
2. What are the factors that affect auditors' evaluation of evidence and, in particular factors affecting the formation of the initial beliefs and the weight assigned to different pieces of evidence?
3. Are there any benefits from following a belief revision approach in auditing particularly benefits related to improving the efficiency and effectiveness of the audit process?

The empirical study depended on two methodologies; a survey research based on personal interviews and an experimental study involving a laboratory experiment. The aims and findings of both the interviews and laboratory experiment are discussed below.

Findings of the Interviews

The survey research depended on personal interviews with practising auditors to collect data about the audit practice concerning the process of evidence evaluation, and factors affecting this process. The limitations of previous studies in this area justified carrying out some personal interviews to explore the audit practice. Precisely, the interviews aimed at addressing the first two research questions.

The interviews were carried out with twelve experienced auditors. Participants were three partners, five senior managers and an internal auditing principal from four of the then 'Big 6' accounting firms, and a partner and two senior managers from a medium-sized firm.

The interviews were analysed to investigate whether auditors follow the belief revision approach in the evidence evaluation process, and the factors affecting this process.

Auditors' approaches in evaluating evidence The analysis of the interviews concerning the evidence evaluation approach came out with the following conclusions:

- The audit steps are the same for both new and continuing clients. However, auditing might take longer with new clients especially that more time is needed at the start of the audit to gather information about the client and the business.
- The formation of initial beliefs is easier with continuing clients than with new ones. Also, the initial beliefs in the case of continuing compared to new clients could be formed at an earlier stage of the audit.
- The size of the client does not have an effect on the formation of initial beliefs. It would only affect the degree of reliance on the internal controls.
- The most important conclusion about the evidence evaluation approach was that the interviewees said that they follow an 'open mind' approach rather than a belief revision one. In other words, in practice auditors do not form an initial belief and then search for evidence to confirm or disconfirm this belief until a final opinion is reached. Even though the interviewees indicated that auditors in practice might have initial beliefs, there is no systematic revision or updating of these beliefs as in the belief revision approach.

It has, therefore, been concluded that with regards to the first research question, auditors in practice do not follow a belief revision approach in their evaluation of evidence. However, some aspects of the belief revision approach might be applicable. The basis that the belief revision approach is built upon is that there is an initial belief. The existence of this initial belief is present even in the open mind approach referred to by the interviewees. However, the concept of this initial belief is debatable and this is discussed further when presenting the findings of the empirical study with regards to the factors affecting auditors' evaluation of evidence.

Furthermore, the finding that the formation of initial beliefs could be easier in the case of continuing clients might have important implications. With continuing clients, auditors might unconsciously have initial beliefs about the financial statements due to their previous involvement with the client. In this case, auditors' behaviour might exhibit a bias toward confirming evidence. However, there is no empirical evidence to support this claim.

The main difference between the belief revision approach and the open mind one, as evidenced from the findings of the interviews, is that auditors in practice do not revise or update their beliefs systematically with pieces of evidence received.

This could possibly explain why the interviewees indicated that they are open-minded. In other words, auditors do not weigh evidence with respect to their beliefs. This is further supported by the analysis of factors affecting auditors' evaluation of evidence.

From the previous discussion, it is concluded that the major finding of the interviews is identifying that practising auditors follow what they label as the 'open mind' approach in evidence evaluation. According to this approach, auditors would start an audit by gathering information about the client and the business. The information that auditors gather with their previous knowledge of the client, in case of continuing ones, help in developing an idea or expectation about the financial statements taking into consideration that most of the auditors' opinions in large accounting firms are clean opinions. Then comes the planning process which includes the risk assessment. Risk assessment itself directs the auditors' attention toward high risk areas and helps in planning the extent of work.

After the planning is done, auditors would proceed to the process of evidence search and evaluation. Auditors are open-minded because evidence is evaluated depending on its nature and source. Auditors' initial beliefs including their ideas, expectations, and risk assessments do not affect the evaluation of evidence.

The audit concludes with forming the final opinion and issuing the audit report. The formation of the final opinion depends on the evidence gathered and is not a result of the revision of the auditors' initial beliefs. Most importantly, the final opinion is not affected by or subject of the initial beliefs.

Factors affecting auditors' evaluation of evidence The interviews were also analysed with respect to factors affecting auditors' evaluation of evidence. Eight factors were considered. These are belief formation, expertise, confirmation bias, professional scepticism, diagnostic content of evidence, evidence order, evaluation mode, and time and cost. Some important results were reached concerning the effects of these factors.

The results of the interviews revealed that there was no agreement about what the interviewees considered to be the initial belief. Three concepts of the initial belief were discussed:
1. Initial beliefs in the form of ideas or assumptions formed during the planning process and based mainly on the previous knowledge of the client.
2. A clean opinion as the initial belief.
3. Risk assessment as the initial belief.

The strongest view was that risk assessment is the initial belief. However, it was indicated that risk assessment is not in itself subject to sequential revisions or updating with pieces of evidence received. This questions the validity of considering risk assessment as the initial belief when following the belief revision approach.

In addition, the interviewees indicated that the initial belief, whatever it is, would mainly be formed by the whole audit team. Although two of the interviewees claimed that the initial beliefs would be formed by the partner or manager, the strongest view was that they would be formed by the whole team. Previous auditing studies indicated that sources of beliefs include self-generated and inherited beliefs. Sources of inherited beliefs include the auditor's superiors, the client's personnel, decision aids, and previous years' working papers. However, none of the previous studies in the area of belief revision referred to the formation of the initial beliefs by the whole audit team and how this might affect the process of evidence evaluation.

Previous auditing studies indicated that when auditors find material changes in the financial statements they form beliefs or expectations about the causes for these changes. These beliefs could take one of two frames; the error frame and the environmental frame. Auditors who put their beliefs in the error frame attribute the causes of material changes to the existence of errors. On the other hand, auditors who put their beliefs in the environmental frame, attribute the causes of material fluctuations to changes in the environment. While the two frames have been referred to by the interviewees in this study, the overwhelming view was that auditors do not form any beliefs or expectations regarding the causes of material fluctuations in the financial statements. The interviewees indicated that they just have to investigate and find out the actual reasons for the changes. Furthermore, one of the interviewees indicated that if material changes existed he would assume that he had missed something in his evaluation.

Expertise has been viewed as an important factor in auditors' search for and evaluation of evidence because experienced auditors are more efficient in their search and can corroborate pieces of evidence easily. However, the team approach would mitigate experience effects.

One of the most important results of the interviews was the fact that auditors do not feel at all committed to their initial belief, if they have one. Consequently, they will not weigh evidence depending on whether it is confirming or disconfirming. Rather, evidence is weighed depending on its source and nature.

The results of the interviews also indicated that auditors are sceptical and cautious particularly with new clients. This scepticism might lead auditors to collect more evidence than needed or it might be reflected in their risk assessment. However, the interviews did not support the idea that professional scepticism or caution would affect the initial belief or auditors' attitudes toward pieces of evidence.

The interviewees preferred to ignore non-diagnostic evidence. However, this result should be taken with caution because the concepts of diagnostic and non-diagnostic evidence are not well established. In fact, the interviewees did not know what is meant by diagnostic evidence, and explanations and examples were given to them. They said that if non-diagnostic evidence is judged as irrelevant evidence or evidence indicating more than one opinion, they would have to ignore it and look for further evidence.

Three main views were expressed by the interviewees about the effect of evidence order. The first view was that the last piece of evidence is the most important piece and, hence, is given more weight. This supports the findings of previous auditing studies and the predictions of the belief-adjustment model about the presence of recency effects. The second view was that order of evidence would be important if pieces of evidence differed in their strength. In other words, if auditors got the strong evidence first, then they might stop looking for other evidence. However, if the strong evidence came later, they would assign more weight to it. The strongest view of the interviewees was that order of evidence is not important and does not affect auditors' decisions.

The results of the interviews indicated that in practice, auditors employ both evidence evaluation modes; the SbS mode and the EoS one. Evidence is first evaluated sequentially and in the end looked at altogether. This has also been supported by what was said about the relationship between the evidence evaluation mode and the level of the auditor. While staff auditors evaluate evidence in a SbS manner, managers look at the evidence gathered less frequently and partners look at the evidence as a whole in the end. It was also indicated that the evidence evaluation mode would depend on the client. If the client provides all the requested information from the outset, then evidence is evaluated in an EoS mode. If not, evidence is evaluated as it arrives. The interviewees also commented that different evidence evaluation modes should not lead to differing opinions.

With regards to time and cost, the interviewees indicated that they work according to a timetable and budget, and that time and cost should not affect the outcomes or effectiveness of the audit process. However, because of the increasing work load and limited time, auditors would be looking for the most efficient way to carry out an audit.

To sum up, the analysis of the interviews regarding the second research question related to factors affecting auditors' evaluation of evidence came out with the following findings:

1. The concept of the initial belief is debatable and the interviewees were not specific about what is considered to be an initial belief.
2. The initial belief, if any, would be formed mainly by the audit team.
3. In conducting analytical review procedures, auditors would not normally form expectations about causes of material fluctuations in the financial statements.
4. The effect of experience on evidence evaluation would be mitigated as a result of the team approach.
5. Auditors do not feel committed to their initial beliefs, if any.
6. Evidence is not classified to confirming and disconfirming with respect to a certain belief.
7. Auditors' scepticism, especially with new clients, is not likely to affect their evidence evaluation.
8. Auditors are likely to ignore non-diagnostic evidence.
9. Order of evidence is not likely to affect auditors' opinions.
10. Both SbS and EoS evaluation modes are employed in practice and should not result in different opinions.
11. Reducing the time and cost of an audit is important as long as this does not affect the outcomes.

The previous findings do not only provide some insight into the audit practice, but they raise some important issues as well. The disagreement about the concept of the initial belief supports the conclusion that auditors in practice do not follow the belief revision approach. Stated differently, the difference in the interviewees opinions about the initial belief indicates that auditors in practice do not consider the process of updating or revising their initial beliefs to be of importance.

Furthermore, carrying out the audit on a team approach basis, and hence the formation of the initial beliefs by the whole audit team, questions studying the effects of different sources of beliefs individually as done by previous studies. In addition, because the work is carried out by the team, this might limit the feeling of commitment to the initial belief and the confirmation (or disconfirmation) bias that could be present in an auditor's individual decision.

The finding that evidence order is not likely to affect auditors' decisions highlights two issues. The first issue relates to whether the order by which evidence is received is controllable by auditors or not. The interviewees indicated that order is not important because the amount of evidence is predetermined. In addition, auditors tend to ask for evidence in a specific order. However, the order by which the evidence arrives might not be controlled by them and depends on factors like whether the client is ready to provide the requested evidence from the outset or not.

The other issue related to evidence order is concerned with the effect of the evidence evaluation approach on the presence of recency effects predicted by the belief-adjustment model and supported by the results of previous auditing studies. These studies supported the presence of recency effects in auditors' decisions when a belief revision approach was employed. However, the findings of the interviews in this study indicated that auditors in practice follow an open mind approach. And, even though, the interviewees indicated that the order of evidence is not likely to affect their decisions. This finding should be considered further especially under the open mind approach.

One of the important findings of the interviews was that related to the evidence evaluation mode. As both SbS and EoS evaluation modes were found to be employed in practice, it becomes necessary to consider the effect of these modes on auditors' opinions. Furthermore, the effect of both evidence evaluation modes should be considered under both the belief revision and open mind approaches.

The finding of the interviews about time and cost highlights the importance of considering the effect of the belief revision approach on the efficiency and effectiveness of the audit process. In this case the belief revision approach should be compared with the open mind approach that the interviewees indicated auditors follow in practice.

Findings of the Experiment

The other part of the empirical study involved a laboratory experiment. The main aim of the experiment was to address the third research question related to whether there are any benefits from following the belief revision approach in auditing.

Beside this main objective, the experiment aimed also at addressing the following questions related to factors affecting auditors' evaluation of evidence:
- Does the change in the evidence evaluation mode affect auditors' decisions?
- Are there any differences between risk assessment and the initial belief?

The objectives of the experiment evolved mainly from the findings of the interviews. The most important finding of the interviews was that auditors in practice follow an open mind approach in their evaluation of evidence. However, auditors might consider any approach that improves the efficiency of the audit without affecting its effectiveness. These findings when linked with the indications in the previous literature that the belief revision approach could improve the efficiency, and even the effectiveness, of the audit process, helped in directing the design of the experiment to find out about the benefits of the belief revision approach. The open mind approach referred to by the interviewees was compared with the belief revision approach to find out whether the two approaches would lead to different results or not.

Two other findings from the interviews were considered in the design of the experimental study. First, the effect of the evidence evaluation mode on the audit process. This effect was considered in both the open mind and belief revision approaches. Second, the concept of the initial belief and how it compares to risk assessment. The comparison between these two concepts has been considered because the strongest view of the interviewees was that risk assessment is their initial belief.

Thus, the experiment was designed to include two independent variables; the evidence evaluation approach and the evaluation mode. Two evidence evaluation approaches were included; the open mind approach and the belief revision one. Two evidence evaluation modes were also included; the SbS mode and the EoS one. This resulted in four experimental groups; open mind SbS (O-SbS), open mind EoS (O-EoS), belief revision SbS (B-SbS), and belief revision EoS (B-EoS).

Subjects were auditors from five of the then 'Big 6' and one medium-sized accounting firm. Overall, 154 experiments were sent out and 64 completed ones were received. Besides, a 'benchmark opinion' was obtained from a group of partners from one of the then 'Big 6' firms. The experimental task was auditing the debtors to arrive at an opinion about the likelihood that they were materially correct.

Analysis of the experiment revealed some important results. Table 8.1 summarises the main results of the experiment. The findings are discussed in terms of the questions that the experimental study addressed.

Table 8.1 Summary of main findings of the experiment

Comparison	Independent Variables	Dependent Variables	Main Results
The efficiency of the belief revision and open mind approaches in the SbS mode	The approach: belief revision and open mind	Experiment time. Expected additional time.	Participants in the belief revision group took significantly less time to complete the experiment. No difference in the expected additional time.
The outcomes of the belief revision and open mind approaches in the SbS mode	The approach: belief revision and open mind	Participants who needed additional work. Participants who arrived at a final opinion. Final opinion %.	More participants in the B-SbS group were able to arrive at a final opinion. No other significant differences.
The efficiency of the belief revision and open mind approaches in the EoS mode	The approach: belief revision and open mind	Experiment time. Expected additional time.	Participants in the belief revision group took significantly less time to complete the experiment. No difference in the expected additional time.
The outcomes of the belief revision and open mind approaches in the EoS mode	The approach: belief revision and open mind	Participants who needed additional work. Participants who arrived at a final opinion. Final opinion %.	No significant differences.
Difference between SbS and EoS modes in the open mind approach	The mode: SbS and EoS	Experiment time. Expected additional time. Participants who needed additional work. Participants who arrived at a final opinion. Final opinion %.	Slight significance in the expected additional time. No other significant differences.

Table 8.1 (continued)

Comparison	Independent Variables	Dependent Variables	Main Results
Difference between SbS and EoS modes in the belief revision approach	The mode: SbS and EoS	Experiment time. Expected additional time. Participants who needed additional work. Participants who arrived at a final opinion. Final opinion %. Belief after evidence from tests of control. Belief after evidence from substantive tests.	No significant differences.
The effectiveness of the belief revision and open mind approachs in the SbS and EoS modes.	Measured by comparing the answers of participants with a 'benchmark opinion'.		No differences between the belief revision and open mind approaches.
Comparing risk assessment and the initial belief in the belief revision groups	Measured by comparing the no. of participants who agreed that risk assessment is the initial belief and those who did not agree and comparing the no. of participants who were able to form an initial belief after reading the background information with those who were not able to do so.		Significantly less participants were able to form an initial belief after reading the background information. No other significant differences.

Efficiency and effectiveness of the belief revision approach The open mind and belief revision approaches were compared to investigate whether the belief revision approach would lead to a more efficient and effective audit or not. The comparisons were carried out once between the belief revision and open mind groups in the SbS mode, and once between the belief revision and open mind groups in the EoS mode.

To find out about the efficiency of the belief revision approach two times were considered; the experiment time and the expected additional time. The results indicated a significant difference in the time of completing the experiment between participants in the open mind group and those in the belief revision group in both evidence evaluation modes. However, the confidence level was higher in the SbS mode. While the difference was significant at 95% confidence level in the SbS mode, it was only significant at 90% in the EoS mode. Comparing the expected additional time required, on the other hand, did not show any significant differences between the open mind and belief revision approaches in both evaluation modes.

The comparison between the belief revision and open mind approaches also involved comparing other outcomes of the experiment. These outcomes included the number of participants who indicated the need for additional work, the number of participants who were able to arrive at a final opinion, and the nature of the final opinion.

The only significant difference that was found was that more participants in the belief revision SbS group (B-SbS) were able to arrive at a final opinion than participants in the open mind SbS group (O-SbS). The result was significant at 90% confidence level. There were no significant differences between the two groups regarding the number of participants who indicated the need for additional work, the number of participants who were able to form a final opinion, and the nature of the final opinion. This might be an indication that employing the belief revision approach is not likely to lead to decisions different from those reached when employing the open mind approach.

Effectiveness, on the other hand, was measured by comparing the results in the open mind and belief revision groups with the 'benchmark opinion'. The comparisons involved the following results:

- Comparing the final opinion.
- Comparing the expected additional work and time.

Most of the participants in all groups were not able to arrive at a final opinion about the materiality of the debtors, which was consistent with the 'benchmark opinion'. No differences were also found between the experimental groups and the 'benchmark opinion' regarding the nature of the additional work needed. With regards to the expected additional time, only the O-EoS group had a mean expected time that was more than that indicated in the 'benchmark opinion' as a result of an extreme estimate of one of the participants in this group. Hence, this difference could not be taken on its own as an indication of the difference between the belief revision and open mind groups regarding the effectiveness of the audit process.

Effectiveness, therefore, did not seem to be affected by the evidence evaluation approach.

It is, therefore, concluded that with regards to the argument in the previous literature that employing the belief revision approach would increase the efficiency and effectiveness of the audit process, the findings of this study provided empirical evidence that efficiency is likely to be improved. On the other hand, effectiveness is not likely to be affected. This finding is of great importance. However, as the results of the interviews indicated that auditors do not employ the belief revision approach, it becomes necessary to consider how far would auditors be willing to employ this approach in their evaluation of evidence. This issue should be considered further because, as indicated from the findings of the interviews, not all aspects of the belief revision approach might be applicable in practice.

The effect of the evidence evaluation mode on auditors' decisions The results of the experiments indicated that there were no significant differences between the SbS and EoS evaluation modes in both the open mind and belief revision groups. This result was reached by taking into consideration a number of dependent variables.

The comparison between the SbS and EoS modes in the open mind approach involved comparing the time of completing the experiment, the expected additional time needed, the number of participants who indicated that additional work is needed, the number of participants who were able to form a final opinion, and the nature of the final opinion.

The comparison between the two evidence evaluation modes in the belief revision approach included in addition to the previous variables comparing the beliefs of participants after evaluating evidence from tests of control and after evaluating evidence from substantive tests.

The results of comparing the evidence evaluation modes showed significant difference in the expected additional time between the O-SbS and O-EoS groups, but only at 89.91% confidence level. Thus, this result should not be taken on its own as an indication that the evidence evaluation mode would affect auditors' decisions especially that in all the other cases the comparison did not reveal any significant difference.

The failure to find a significant difference between the SbS and EoS modes is an indication that the difference in the evidence evaluation mode is not likely to affect auditors' decisions. This result is important to the audit practice and should be considered further especially that the interviewees indicated that both SbS and EoS modes are employed.

The difference between risk assessment and the initial belief The comparison of risk assessment with the initial belief indicated that there is no agreement as to whether risk assessment is the initial belief or not. While some participants regarded risk assessment as their initial belief, others did not agree. No significant difference was found between the two views. Furthermore, most of the participants who provided their risk assessment put it in the form of high, medium, or low without differentiation between the components of risk. This supports the findings of the interviews that risk is assessed subjectively as an overall assessment.

The disagreement among the participants about the relationship between risk assessment and the initial belief when linked with the results of the interviews raises two important issues. First, the comparison between risk and belief and how it affects auditors' perception of the concept of the initial belief. Second, the difference between the audit risk model and the belief-adjustment model.

The first issue concerns the comparison between risk and belief. This issue emerges mainly from the results of the interviews and the varying abilities of the interviewees to reflect on these concepts. The answers of the interviewees reveal the vagueness associated with the concept of an initial belief. While some of the interviewees regarded their ideas, assumptions, or expectations as their initial beliefs, most of them considered risk assessment to be the initial belief.

In considering risk to be the initial belief, the interviewees did not seem to have a clear understanding that an initial belief is revised with pieces of evidence gathered until a final opinion is reached which is issued in the audit report. Risk assessment in this case could not be considered as an initial belief. Risk assessment, as mentioned by the interviewees, directs the attention toward areas of high risk and, thus, helps in determining the extent of work. As indicated by SAS 300 and by the interviewees, risk assessment is revised only if information comes to the auditors' attention that differs significantly from the information on which they originally assessed risk. In this sense, the revision of risk assessment would result in a change in the planned substantive procedures but not in a revision of an opinion. Hence, risk assessment would not lead in the end to the final opinion issued in the audit report.

It might be also of relevance here to consider the difference between a belief and the strength of that belief. While the belief is an expression of a certain opinion, the strength of the belief is how strongly someone believes in his/her opinion. This distinction was implicitly indicated by Hogarth and Einhorn (1992). The difficulty in agreeing about the concept of the initial belief by the interviewees also reveals that they do not have a clear distinction between a belief and the strength of that belief. For example, in saying that a clean opinion is the initial belief, this does not indicate the strength that auditors believe to have a clean opinion.

In the belief revision approach, it is assumed that auditors when forming an initial belief would determine both the belief and the strength of that belief. This is revealed in the experimental study by asking participants in the belief revision groups to form their initial expectation which consists of their idea that debtors are materially correct (the belief) and the percentage by which they believe debtors are materially correct (the strength of the belief). A revision of this expectation by pieces of evidence would lead to the formation of the final opinion about the materiality of the debtors.

The previous discussion indicates that while the revision of the initial belief would lead to a final opinion, the revision of risk assessment would not. Hence, it is difficult to consider risk as the initial belief. This conclusion reveals the vagueness in the concept of an initial belief displayed in both the answers of the interviewees and the results of the experiment. While most of the interviewees regarded risk assessment to be their initial belief, this might not hold true. In addition, the results of the experiment indicated that some participants viewed risk assessment to be their initial belief while others did not and no significant difference between the two views was present. This supports the need for further research on the concept of the initial belief in auditing and how it relates to risk assessment.

The other issue that emerges from the comparison of risk and belief in both the interviews and experiment is the difference between the audit risk model and the belief-adjustment model. The audit risk model is used to measure the audit risk for a particular account where:

Audit Risk = Inherent Risk × Control Risk × Detection Risk

The audit risk model is, therefore, employed by practising auditors to assess risk if the components of risk could be quantified. Otherwise, risk is assessed subjectively as high, medium, or low which is more likely to happen in audit practice as indicated by the results of the interviews and experiment.

The belief-adjustment model, on the other hand, has a different objective than the audit risk model. The belief-adjustment model introduced by Hogarth and Einhorn (1992) is used in measuring belief revisions. It is considered as a descriptive theory of belief updating (Hogarth and Einhorn, 1992, p. 2). In this sense, the belief-adjustment model is a descriptive model. A descriptive model "embodies or explicates a theory that explains and/or predicts empirical phenomena: explanation so as to understand observed events and/or prediction so as to anticipate and perhaps control future events (Waller and Jiambalvo, 1984, p. 202).

The difference between the audit risk model and the belief-adjustment model means that the belief-adjustment model could not substitute the audit risk model even if auditors employed the belief revision approach in their evaluation of evidence. In fact, the belief-adjustment model is a model to be employed by researchers interested in studying the belief revision approach and predictions related to this approach. The belief-adjustment model is not a model to be employed by practising auditors, for instance, to measure risk even if the various components of risk could be quantified.

Perhaps the previous distinction between the audit risk model and belief-adjustment model also supports the view that it might not be reasonable to consider risk assessment as the initial belief which stresses on the need for further research on comparing risk assessment and the initial belief.

The analysis of the experiment also showed significant difference between the number of participants who were able to form an initial belief and those who were not. The majority of the participants were not able to form an initial belief after reading the background information and before being presented with pieces of evidence, which points out to the difficulty of forming an initial belief at an early stage of the audit process. This supports the findings of the interviews that the formation of initial beliefs is difficult in the case of new clients especially that the experimental task could be considered as a new client to the participants.

Implications of the Findings of the Empirical Study

The empirical study came out with findings that might have implications on academics, policy makers, and practitioners. However, it should be noted before discussing the implications that the findings relate to a relatively routine task via the debtors' audit. Hence, these findings might not hold for other audit tasks.

Implications of the Findings on Academics

The findings of this study highlight two important implications on academics/researchers. First, the domination of laboratory experiments in studies in the area of belief revision and how this leads to a gap between audit practice and the literature. Second the need of studies on auditors' evaluation of evidence.

Previous auditing studies in the area of belief revision assumed that auditors follow a belief revision approach in practice. This assumption was based mainly on research findings in the area of psychology. The previous auditing studies depended mainly on laboratory experiments where the conditions of the experiments were set to reveal belief revision behaviour. Precisely, subjects of previous studies were asked to form an initial belief and then update it with subsequent pieces of evidence, which does not reveal the audit practice as evidenced from the results of the interviews.

The laboratory form of experimentation was relevant to the purposes of the previous studies, whether they aimed at investigating the presence of recency effects or the factors affecting auditors' beliefs and attitudes toward evidence. However, the main drawback of laboratory experiments is that they do not allow for describing the audit practice.

The reason that previous research depended on laboratory experiments could be attributed mainly to the fact that belief revision falls under the category of information processing. Research in the area of information processing is still not well-established and, even though, methodological tools like experiments and statistics are employed, one cannot directly observe the phenomena of interest (Hogarth, 1991). This is the reason that studies in the area of information processing depend on observing the inputs and outputs (Hogarth, 1991). The observation of the inputs and outputs takes the form of investigating the cause-effect relationship, which is best carried out by laboratory experiments.

However, the dominance of laboratory experiments in the area of information processing should not affect the use of other methodologies, like survey research, that could be employed to describe and investigate the practice. Survey research could also be very important to direct the design of laboratory experiments that are still needed in studies concerned with the cause-effect relationship.

This study made an attempt to understand the audit practice in relation to evidence evaluation. Such attempt was made by carrying out personal interviews with experienced auditors. The findings revealed that auditors in practice do not follow the belief revision approach in their evaluation of evidence. Rather, an open mind approach is followed.

The belief revision approach implies a very systematic way of evidence evaluation; forming an initial belief then revising or updating it with subsequent pieces of evidence until a final opinion is reached. The results of the interviews indicated that evidence search and evaluation are not carried out in this systematic pattern. The results also indicated that many of the issues addressed by previous studies might not hold true or might not be the concern of audit practitioners.

Although this study was carried out in the UK and the previous studies were mostly American studies, the way of carrying out an audit is not likely to differ between countries. This, consequently, puts doubt on the applicability of psychological research findings to audit settings. Although individuals in general might exhibit a belief revision behaviour, auditors, on the other hand, might not employ this behaviour in carrying out an audit.

The findings of the interviews also indicated that forming initial beliefs with continuing clients might be easier and could be formed at an earlier stage of the audit than with new clients. Although this finding is very important in studying auditors' belief revisions, it was not considered by previous studies. When studying auditors' belief revisions in a laboratory setting, the case or scenario provided to participants could be considered as a new client to them. In this case, the results are better explained in terms of new audit engagements. This raises the issue of whether auditors' belief revisions would differ in the case of continuing clients compared to new ones. In other words, would the findings of previous studies concerning the existence of recency effects and auditors' attitudes toward confirming and disconfirming evidence hold true in the case of continuing clients.

This study depended also on employing a laboratory experiment. However, the design and aims of the experiment were directed by the findings of the interviews. The experiment was designed to investigate the differences between the belief revision approach and the open mind one. The design of the experiment to include both the belief revision and open mind approaches could not have been done without carrying out the interviews in the first place. In fact, the existence of the open mind approach has been revealed as a result of the interviews.

To conclude, although laboratory experiments are of great benefit in the area of information processing to investigate the effect of certain inputs on the outcomes, there is a need to employ other methodologies, like survey research, to describe and investigate the audit practice.

The second implication related to academic researchers is the lack of auditing research especially in the UK concerning evidence evaluation. In a comparison between auditing research in the US and that in the UK, Gwilliam (1987) indicated that auditing research in the UK has been limited and slow to develop compared to the US research. Gwilliam (1987) also concluded that even though there are environmental and regulatory differences between the US and the UK, many US audit research findings would be applicable to the UK. However, he added that the differences between the two countries still need to be taken into account.

The conclusion here is the need of more UK auditing research not only in the area of evidence search and evaluation, but in auditing in general.

Implications of the Findings on Policy Makers

According to the findings of this study, there are three number of issues that need to be considered by policy makers. These issues are related to auditing standards concerned with evidence, analytical procedures, and risk assessment.

The auditing standards issued by the Auditing Practices Board in the UK and concerned with evidence provide guidance on the quantity and quality of evidence. SAS 400.1 indicates that evidence should be sufficient and appropriate. Although SAS 400.2 indicates that evidence should support the assessed level of control risk and SAS 400.3 indicates that evidence should support the financial statement assertions, no guidance was provided about the approach of evidence evaluation.

Providing guidance on the way auditors should approach evidence is of great help to practitioners especially that evidence search and evaluation are the centre of the audit process. The findings of the empirical study indicated that although auditors do not follow the belief revision approach in their evaluation of evidence, this approach is more efficient than the open mind approach. This result questions the lack of auditing standards to guide the process of evidence search and evaluation.

In addition, the findings of the interviews indicated that auditors in practice do not form beliefs regarding the expected causes of significant fluctuations in the financial statements. Rather, auditors have to investigate and search for the actual reasons. This approach is consistent with SAS 410.4 on investigating fluctuations or unexpected relationships. However, it is not consistent with the US SAS 56 on analytical procedures. This difference raises two important questions. First, how far does the difference in the auditing standards between the US and the UK affect the audit practice. This also leads to the consideration of the issue raised by Gwilliam (1987) about the applicability of the US research findings to the UK.

The other important question that should be considered by policy makers is concerned with the reasons for the difference between the US and the UK standards. The importance of this issue comes also from the fact that the 'Big 5' accounting firms operate in both the US and the UK. Thus, it becomes important to consider whether the difference in the standards reveals the difference in the practice or not. It also becomes of interest to consider whether the 'Big 5' accounting firms perform differently in the UK compared to the US due to the difference in the standards. As an example, would US auditors form expectations when conducting analytical procedures while UK auditors do not due to the difference between the US SAS 56 and the UK SAS 410.4?

In addition, this study also revealed the fuzziness associated with risk assessment. While some participants in the experimental study agreed that risk is assessed as the likeliness of the debtors to be materially correct, others indicated that risk is assessed either as high, normal, or low. The latter view is consistent with the results of the interviews. The results indicate that the view to risk assessment in practice is not the structured view of risk as indicated in the auditing standards.

The auditing standards concerned with risk assessment (SASs 300.1, 300.2, and 300.7) indicate that auditors should assess the components of audit risk including inherent, control, and detection risks. However, in practice auditors did not show any differentiation between the components of risk. This points out to an important issue to be considered by policy makers and relates to the consideration of the audit practice in the issuance of the auditing standards.

Implications of the Findings on Practitioners

There are two important implications on audit practitioners. The first implication relates to the employment of the belief revision approach in evidence evaluation. The second implication concerns the funding of auditing research by UK accounting firms.

Auditors are always concerned about the efficiency and effectiveness of the audit process. Efficiency, nowadays, is extremely important because of the high work load on auditors. This highlights the increasing pressure on auditors to complete their audit work in less time without affecting the quality of the work.

The results of this study showed that employing the belief revision approach enabled auditors to complete their experimental task in less time without affecting the final outcome. This result is of great importance to the audit practice. The study found that practising auditors follow an open mind approach in their evaluation of evidence. At the same time, they are concerned with the time limit due to the increasing work load these days. This means that auditors could reduce the time needed to complete an audit by changing their approach in evaluating evidence.

Although the aspects of the belief revision approach as described in the auditing literature might not all be relevant in practice, the broad concept of the approach could be employed. The study revealed that auditors in practice do not weigh evidence depending on whether it is confirming or not. Evidence is always weighed depending on its source and nature. However, auditors could still be able to form an initial belief and then update it with pieces of evidence received. The belief revision approach is particularly efficient in the case of a SbS evaluation of evidence. As it has been argued by Hogarth and Einhorn (1992), the process of revising the belief after evaluating each piece of evidence reduces memory load. In addition, this could also reduce the need to go back to working papers to incorporate the new piece of evidence with all the ones. Rather, the auditor at any time will deal only with the current belief and one piece of evidence.

There are also other indications in the audit literature that auditors have problem in integrating and remembering pieces of evidence. Moeckel (1990) for example found that auditors, especially inexperienced auditors, have problems in integrating evidence. In other words, auditors sometimes fail to make connections between pieces of evidence received separately and formulate a meaning of all evidence together. Church (1990) also said that auditors might have inaccurate memories of evidence that has been collected. He added that sometimes because of time pressures or auditors' confidence in themselves, they might rely on their inaccurate memories instead of going back to working papers. The failure to integrate and remember pieces of evidence could be resolved by employing the belief revision approach.

In the belief revision approach, evidence is evaluated with respect to the belief under consideration and, hence, it becomes easier to integrate pieces of evidence. In addition, as has previously been stated, the auditor at any one time deals with the current belief and one piece of evidence. These benefits together with findings of this study that the belief revision approach might improve the efficiency of the audit process, make it relevant for practitioners to consider employing this approach.

The other implication on practitioners relates to the funding of auditing research by UK accounting firms. One of the reasons that Gwilliam (1987) states as a factor of the limited UK auditing research compared to the US is that in the US accounting firms provide funds to support the auditing research. They also provide support in terms of access to personnel, data, and introductions to clients. However, in the UK this support from accounting firms is limited.

Areas for Future Research

The limitations and findings of this study highlight a number of issues that could be areas for future research.

The results of the interviews and experiment are limited because of the relatively small number of participants and because there are no other studies to corroborate the findings especially those related to the effect of employing the belief revision approach on the efficiency of the audit process.

In addition, the experimental study was originally intended to be carried out in one of the then 'Big 6' accounting firms. The senior manager, from this 'Big 6' firm, who reviewed the experimental instrument re-phrased the task to be 'checking that debtors are materially correct'. Because of the low response rate, participation in the experiment was sought from other firms. It should, therefore, be noted that auditors from different firms (and possibly those from the same firm) might not have perceived materiality to be the same. This might have confounded the results especially in relation to the participants' ability to form an initial belief.

The previous limitations suggest the need for further research to investigate the benefits of the belief revision approach and to provide more insight into the audit practice concerning evidence evaluation.

Further research is also needed in the area of risk assessment and how it relates to the initial belief because of the importance of this issue to the belief revision approach.

The experimental study depended on the task of auditing the debtors which suggests the need for further research in other auditing tasks. The effect of employing the belief revision approach on auditors' decisions in other auditing tasks, especially in analytical review tasks, is in need of investigation. Precisely, the formation of beliefs about causes of unexpected fluctuations and how this would affect the subsequent search for and evaluation of evidence is in need of further research. This issue needs to be considered especially in a UK auditing context because the findings of the interviews indicated that auditors do not form expectations about causes of material fluctuations in the financial statements.

In addition, the task of auditing the debtors is a relatively routine task. This means that the findings might not hold true for other auditing tasks that require a *holistic* understanding of the business like going concern and fraud. For these areas an open mind approach is, *prima facie*, more likely to be effective which suggests the need for further research to investigate this issue.

The way auditors corroborate evidence, especially contradictory evidence, according to the open mind approach is in need of further research. Even though the interviewees explained how they would approach evidence evaluation in practice, the way they integrate pieces of evidence together to form an opinion needs further investigation. In relation to this point, it would be worth examining other areas of literature like law, education, and philosophy, which might provide deeper understanding of the concept of open-mindedness in evidence evaluation.

Another issue related to the open mind approach is the effect of evidence order on auditors' decisions. This issue was investigated by previous studies in case of employing the belief revision approach. Even though the interviewees indicated that the order of evidence is not likely to affect their decisions, it would be worth investigating, by experimentation, the cause-effect relationship between evidence order and auditors' decisions in the case of an open mind approach.

An important issue that should also be considered further is the team approach and its effect on auditors' decisions. The findings of the interviews revealed that most of the audit work is done on a team basis particularly in large, or even medium-sized, accounting firms. This could provide a possible explanation of why the interviewees indicated that they would not be committed to their initial beliefs, if any, and would not classify evidence to confirming and disconfirming. On the other hand, previous auditing studies that investigated auditors' attitudes toward evidence did this on an individual basis. This suggests the need for considering the validity of the findings of previous studies when the decisions are formed by the audit team rather than individual auditors.

Another area for future research is considering the applicability of the belief revision approach. The findings of the experiment indicated that employing the belief revision approach in evidence evaluation might be of benefit to the efficiency of the audit process. Thus, it would be worth investigating how far would practising auditors be accepting to employ the belief revision approach.

Research is also required to further investigate whether the open mind approach is an alternative pattern of behaviour, or the case is just that auditors are unconscious to what they do. It is interesting, however, to note that even if auditors were found to unconsciously follow the belief revision behaviour, that they reject such behaviour and consider it to be biased.

To conclude, although this study provided some insight concerning the audit practice in relation to evidence evaluation, and the effect of employing the belief revision approach on the audit process, a number of issues are still in need of further investigation and provide fruitful areas for future research.

Bibliography

Abou-Seada, M. (1999), *The Effect of Using the Belief Revision Approach on Auditors' Decision-Making during their Search for and Evaluation of Evidence*, Unpublished PhD thesis, University of the West of England, Bristol.

Adams, G. R. and Schvaneveldt, J. D. (1991), *Understanding Research Methods*, 2nd edition, Longman, New York.

Akresh, A. D., Loebbecke, J. K. and Scott, W. R. (1988), Audit Approaches and Techniques, In: *Research Opportunities in Auditing: The Second Decade*, Abdel-khalik, A. R. and Solomon, I. (eds.), American Accounting Association: Auditing Section, pp. 13-55.

American Institute of Certified Public Accountants (1988), *Statement on Auditing Standards No. 56: Analytical Procedures*, New York, AICPA.

Anderson, B. H. and Maletta, M. (1994), Auditor attendance to negative and positive information: the effect of experience-related differences, *Behavioral Research in Accounting*, Vol. 6, pp. 1-20.

Anderson, J. R. (1982), Acquisition of cognitive skill, *Psychological Review*, Vol. 89, No. 4, pp. 369-406.

Anderson, U. and Koonce, L. (1995), Explanation as a method for evaluating client-suggested causes in analytical procedures, *Auditing: A Journal of Practice and Theory*, Vol. 14, No. 2, Fall, pp. 124-131.

Asare, S. K. (1992), The auditor's going-concern decision: Interaction of task variables and the sequential processing of evidence, *The Accounting Review*, Vol. 67, No. 2, April, pp. 379-393.

Ashton, A. H. and Ashton, R. H. (1988), Sequential belief revision in auditing, *The Accounting Review*, Vol. 63, No. 4, October, pp. 623-641.

Ashton, R. H. and Ashton, A. H. (1990), Evidence-responsiveness in professional judgement: effects of positive versus negative evidence and presentation mode, *Organizational Behavior and Human Decision Processes*, Vol. 46, pp. 1-19.

Ashton, R. H. and Brown, P. R. (1980), Descriptive modelling of auditors' internal control judgments: replication and extension, *Journal of Accounting Research*, Spring, pp. 269-277.

Ashton, R. H., Kleinmuntz, D. N., Sullivan, J. B. and Tomassini, L. A. (1988), Audit decision making, In: *Research Opportunities in Auditing: The Second Decade*, Abdel-khalik, A. R. and Solomon, I. (eds.), American Accounting Association, Auditing Section, pp. 95-132.

Auditing Practices Board (1995), *Statement of Auditing Standards SAS 200: Planning*, March, APB.

Auditing Practices Board (1995), *Statement of Auditing Standards SAS 300.1(b): Accounting and Internal Control Systems and Audit Risk Assessments*, March, APB.

Auditing Practices Board (1995), *Statement of Auditing Standards SAS 300.2: Inherent Risk*, March, APB.

Auditing Practices Board (1995), *Statement of Auditing Standards SAS 300.4: Control Risk*, March, APB.

Auditing Practices Board (1995), *Statement of Auditing Standards SAS 300.7: Detection Risk*, March, APB.

Auditing Practices Board (1995), *Statement of Auditing Standards SAS 300, para 55: Accounting and Internal Control Systems and Audit Risk Assessments*, March, APB.

Auditing Practices Board (1995), *Statement of Auditing Standards SAS 400.1: Audit Evidence*, March, APB.

Auditing Practices Board (1995), *Statement of Auditing Standards SAS 400.2: Tests of Control*, March, APB.

Auditing Practices Board (1995), *Statement of Auditing Standards SAS 400.3: Substantive Procedures*, March, APB.

Auditing Practices Board (1995), *Statement of Auditing Standards SAS 410.4: Investigating Significant Fluctuations or Unexpected Relationships*, March, APB.

Ayers, S. and Kaplan, S. E. (1993), An examination of the effect of hypothesis framing on auditors' information choices in an analytical procedure task, *ABACUS*, Vol. 29, No. 2, pp. 113-129.

Bamber, E. M., Ramsay, R. J. and Tubbs, R. M. (1997), An examination of the descriptive validity of the belief-adjustment model and alternative attitudes to evidence in auditing, *Accounting, Organizations and Society*, Vol. 22, Nos. 3/4, pp. 249-268.

Bedard, J. (1989), Expertise in auditing, *Accounting, Organizations and Society*, Vol. 14, Nos. 1/2, 113-131.

Bedard, J. and Biggs, S. F. (1991), Pattern recognition, hypotheses generation, and auditor performance in an analytical task, *The Accounting Review*, Vol. 66, No. 3, July, pp. 622-642.

Bedard, J. and Chi, M. T. H. (1993), Expertise in auditing, *Auditing: A Journal of Practice and Theory*, Vol. 12, Supplement, pp. 21-45.

Biggs, S. and Mock, T. (1983), An investigation of auditor decision processes in the evaluation of internal controls and audit scope decisions, *Journal of Accounting Research*, Spring, pp. 234-255.

Bonner, S. E. and Lewis, B. L. (1990), Determinants of auditor expertise, *Journal of Accounting Research*, Vol. 28, Supplement, pp. 1-20.

Boritz, J. E. (1986), The effect of research method on audit planning and review judgments, *Journal of Accounting Research*, Vol. 26, No.2, Autumn, pp. 335-348.

Bouwman, M. J. (1984), Expert vs novice decision making in accounting: a summary, *Accounting, Organizations and Society*, Vol. 9, June, pp. 325-327.

Butt, J. L. and Campbell, T. L. (1989), The effects of information order and hypothesis-testing strategies on auditors' judgments, *Accounting, Organizations and Society*, Vol. 14, No. 5/6, pp. 471-479.

Christ, M. Y. (1993), Evidence on the nature of audit planning problem representations: an examination of auditor free recalls, *The Accounting Review*, Vol. 68, No. 2, April, pp. 304-322.

Chung, J. and Monroe, G. (1996), *The Effects of Counterexplanation and Source of Hypothesis on Audit Judgment*, Paper presented at the British Accounting Association National Conference, Cardiff.

Church, B. K. (1990), Auditors' use of confirmatory processes, *Journal of Accounting Literature*, Vol. 9, pp. 81-112.

Church, B. K. (1991), An examination of the effect that commitment to a hypothesis has on auditors' evaluations of confirming and disconfirming evidence, *Contemporary Accounting Research*, Vol. 7, No. 2, Spring, pp. 513-534.

Church, B. K. and Schneider, A. (1993), Auditors' generation of diagnostic hypotheses in response to a superior's suggestion: interference effects, *Contemporary Accounting Research*, Vol. 10, No. 1, Fall, pp. 333-350.

Colbert, J. L. (1989), The effect of experience on auditors' judgments, *Journal of Accounting Literature,* Vol. 8, pp. 137-149.

Coolican, H. (1994), *Research Methods and Statistics in Psychology*, 2nd edition, Hodder and Stoughton, London.

Cramer, D. (1994), *Introducing Statistics for Social Research: Step-by-Step Calculations and Computer Techniques Using SPSS*, Routledge, London.

Cresswell, J. (1994), *Research Design: Qualitative and Quantitative Approaches*, Sage Publications, Inc., Thousand Oaks, California.

Cushing, B. E. and Ahlawat, S. S. (1996), Mitigation of recency bias in audit judgment: the effect of documentation, *Auditing: A Journal of Practice and Theory*, Vol. 15, No. 2, Fall, pp. 110-122.

Cushing, B. E. and Leobbecke, J. K. (1986), *A Comparison of Audit Methodologies of Large Accounting Firms*, Studies in Accounting Research No. 26, American Accounting Association, Sarasota, Florida.

Darly, J. M. and Gross, P. H. (1983), A hypothesis-confirming bias in labelling effects, *Journal of Personality and Social Psychology*, Vol. 44, No. 1, pp. 20-33.

Davidson, P. and Wahlund, R. (1992), A note on the failure to use negative information, *Journal of Economic Psychology*, Vol. 13, pp. 343-353.

Davis, J. S. and Solomon, I. (1989), Experience, expertise, and expert-performance research in public accounting, *Journal of Accounting Literature*, Vol. 8, pp. 150-164.

Dillard, J. F., Kauffman, N. L. and Spires, E. E. (1991), Evidence order and belief revision in management accounting, *Accounting, Organizations and Society*, Vol. 16, No. 7, pp. 619-633.

Dobbins, G. H., Lane, I. M. and Steiner, D. D. (1988), A note on the role of laboratory methodologies in applied behavioral research: don't throw out the baby with the bath water, *Journal of Organizational Behavior*, Vol. 9, pp. 281-286.

Easterby-Smith, M., Thorpe, R. and Lowe, A. (1991), *Management Research: An Introduction*, Sage Publications Ltd., London.

Edwards, W. (1968), Conservatism in Human Information Processing, In: *Formal Representations of Human Judgment*, Kleinmuntz, B. (ed.), Wiley, New York, pp. 17-52.

Einhorn, H. (1976), A synthesis: accounting and behavioral research, *Journal of Accounting Research*, Supplement, pp. 196-206.

Einhorn, H. J. and Hogarth, R. M. (1985), *A contrast/surprise model for updating beliefs*, University of Chicago, Graduate School of Business, Center for Decision Research, April.

Einhorn, H. J. and Hogarth, R. M. (1987), *Adaption and Inertia in Belief Updating: The Contrast-Inertia Model*, Working Paper, Center for Decision Research, University of Chicago, October.

Elstein, A. S., Shulman, L. S. and Sprafka, S. A. (1978), *Medical Problem Solving: An Analysis of Clinical Reasoning*, Harvard University Press.

Evans, J. (1987), Beliefs and expectations as causes of judgmental bias, In: *Judgmental Forecasting*, Wright, G. and Ayton, P. (eds.), New York, John Wiley and Sons, pp. 31-47.

Felix, W. L., Jr. and Kinney, W. R., Jr. (1982), Research in the auditor's formulation process: state of the art, *The Accounting Review*, Vol. 57, April, pp. 245-271.

Frankfort-Nachmias, C. and Nachmias, D. (1992), *Research Methods in the Social Sciences*, 4th edition, Edward Arnold, London.

Frensch, P. A. and Sternberg, R. J. (1989), Expertise and intelligent thinking: when is it worse to know better, In: *Advances in the Psychology of Human Intelligence*, Sternberg, R. (ed.), Erlbaum, Hillsdale, New Jersey, pp. 157-188.

Gibbins, M. (1984), Propositions about the psychology of professional judgment in public accounting, *Journal of Accounting Research*, Vol. 22, Spring, pp. 103-125.

Gibbons, J. (1993), *Nonparametric Statistics: An Introduction*, Sage Publications, London.

Glover, S. M. (1997), The influence of time pressure and accountability on auditors' processing of nondiagnostic information, *Journal of Accounting Research*, Vol. 35, No. 2, Autumn, pp. 213-237.

Glynn, J. J. (1985), *Value for Money Auditing in the Public Sector*, Prentice-Hall International, Englewood Cliffs, New Jersey, in association with The Institute of Chartered Accountants in England and Wales.

Gwilliam, D. (1987), *A Survey of Auditing Research*, Prentice-Hall International, Englewood Cliffs, New Jersey, in association with The Institute of Chartered Accountants in England and Wales.

Hackenbrack, K. (1992), Implications of seemingly irrelevant evidence in audit judgments, *Journal of Accounting Research*, Vol. 30, No. 1, Spring, pp. 126-136.

Hastie, R. (1980), Memory for behavioral information that confirms or contradicts a personality impression, In: *Person Memory: The Cognitive Basis of Social Perception*, Hastie, R., Ostrom, T., Ebbesen, E., Wyer, R., Hamilton, D. and Carlston, D. (eds.), Hillsdale, New Jersey, Lawrence Erlbaum Publishers, pp. 155-177.

Hatherly, D. (1980), *The Audit Evidence Process*, Anderson Keenan Publishing, London.

Hatherly, D., Brown, T. and Innes, J. (1998), Free-form reporting and perceptions of the audit, *British Accounting Review*, Vol. 30, pp. 23-38.

Heiman-Hoffman, V. B., Moser, D. V. and Joseph, J. A. (1995), The impact of auditor's initial hypothesis on subsequent performance at identifying actual errors, *Contemporary Accounting Research*, Vol. 11, No. 2, Spring, pp. 763-779.

Higson, A. (1997), Developments in audit approaches: from audit efficiency to audit effectiveness, In: *Current Issues in Auditing*, Sherer, M. and Turley, S. (editors), 3rd edition, Paul Chapman Publishing Ltd., London, pp. 198-215.

Hirst, D. E. and Koonce, L. (1996), Audit analytical procedures: a field investigation, *Contemporary Accounting Research*, Vol. 13, No. 2, Fall, pp. 457-486.

Hogarth, R. M. (1991), A perspective on cognitive research in accounting, *The Accounting Review*, Vol. 66, No. 2, April, pp. 277-290.

Hogarth, R. M. and Einhorn, H. J. (1992), Order effects in belief updating: the belief-adjustment model, *Cognitive Psychology*, 24, pp. 1-55.

Hooper, C. and Trotman, K. T. (1996), Configural information processing in auditing: Further evidence, *Accounting and Business Research*, Vol. 26, No. 2, pp. 125-136.

Humphry, C. and Moizer, P. (1990), From techniques to ideologies: an alternative perspective on the audit function, *Critical Perspectives on Accounting*, Vol. 1, pp. 217-238.

Hussey, J. and Hussey, R. (1997), *Business Research: A Practical Guide for Undergraduate and Postgraduate Students*, Macmillan Business, London.

Innes, J., Brown, T. and Hatherly, D. (1997), The expanded audit report - a research study within the development of SAS 600, *Accounting, Auditing and Accountability Journal*, Vol. 10, No. 5, pp. 702-717.

Ismail, Z. and Trotman, K. T. (1995), The impact of the review process in hypothesis generation tasks, *Accounting, Organizations and Society*, Vol. 20, No. 5, pp. 345-357.

Joyce, E. J. (1976), Expert judgment in audit program planning, *Human Information Processing in Accounting*, pp. 29-60.

Kaplan, S. E. and Reckers, P. M. J. (1989), An examination of information search during initial audit planning, *Accounting, Organizations and Society*, Vol. 14, No. 5/6, pp. 539-550.

Kaplan, S. E., Moeckel, C. and Williams, J. D. (1992), Auditors' hypothesis plausibility assessments in an analytical review setting, *Auditing: A Journal of Practice and Theory*, Vol. 11, No. 2, Fall, pp. 50-65.

Kennedy, J. (1993), Debiasing audit judgment with accountability: a framework and experimental results, *Journal of Accounting Research*, Vol. 31, No. 2, Autumn, pp. 231-245.

Kerr, D. S. and Ward, D. D. (1994), The effects of audit task on evidence integration and belief revision, *Behavioral Research in Accounting*, Vol. 6, pp. 21-42.

Kervin, J. B. (1992), *Methods for Business Research*, Harper Collins Publishers, New York.

Kida, T. (1984), The impact of hypothesis-testing strategies on auditors' use of judgment data, *Journal of Accounting Research*, Vol. 22, No. 1, Spring, pp. 332-340.

King, R. D. and O'Keefe, T. B. (1989), Belief revision from hypothesis testing, *Journal of Accounting Literature*, Vol. 8, pp. 1-24.

Kirkham, L. M. (1992), Putting auditing practices in context: deciphering the message in auditor responses to selected environmental cues, *Critical Perspectives on Accounting*, Vol. 3, pp. 291-314.

Klayman, J. and Ha, Y. (1987), Confirmation, disconfirmation, and information in hypothesis testing, *Psychological Review*, Vol. 94, No. 2, pp. 211-228.

Knechel, W. R. and Messier, W. F., Jr. (1990), Sequential auditor decision making: information search and evidence evaluation, *Contemporary Accounting Research*, Vol. 6, No. 2-I, pp. 386-406.

Koonce, L. (1993), A cognitive charaterization of audit analytical review, *Auditing: A Journal of Practice and Theory*, Vol. 12, Supplement, pp. 57-76.

Koonce, L. and Phillips, F. (1996), Auditors' comprehension and evaluation of client-suggested causes in analytical procedures, *Behavioral Research in Accounting*, Vol. 8, pp. 32-48.

Krishnamoorthy, G., Wright, A. and Cohen, J. (1997), Evidence on the effect of financial and non-financial trends on hypothesis generation, available on www.indiana.edu/~audsec/98midyr/Ganesh.html, July.

Krogstad, J. L., Ettenson, R. T. and Shanteau, J. (1984), Context and experience in auditors' materiality judgments, *Auditing: A Journal of Practice and Theory*, Fall, pp. 54-73.

Krull, G., Jr., Reckers, P. M. J. and Wong-On-Wing, B. (1993), The effect of experience, fraudulent signals and information presentation order on auditors' beliefs, *Auditing: A Journal of Practice and Theory*, Vol. 12, No. 2, Fall, pp. 143-153.

Libby, R. (1981), *Accounting and Human Information Processing: Theory and Applications*, Prentice-Hall, Englewood Cliffs, New Jersey.

Libby, R. (1985), Availability and the generation of hypotheses in analytical review, *Journal of Accounting Research,* Autumn, pp. 648-667.
Maltby, J. (1996), *Cases in Auditing*, 2nd edition, Paul Chapman Publishing Ltd., London.
Marchant, G. (1989), Analogical reasoning and hypothesis generation in auditing, *The Accounting Review*, Vol. 64, No. 3, July, pp. 500-513.
Mautz, R. K. and Sharaf, H. A. (1961), *The Philosophy of Auditing*, Monograph No. 6, American Accounting Association, Florida.
McMillan, J. J. and White, R. A. (1993), Auditors' belief revisions and evidence search: the effect of hypothesis frame, confirmation bias, and professional skepticism, *The Accounting Review*, Vol. 68, No. 3, July, pp. 443-465.
McMillan, J. J. and White, R. A. (1996), A reexamination of auditors' initial belief assessment and evidence search, *Advances in Accounting*, Vol. 14, pp. 193-208.
Messier, W. F., Jr. (1992), The sequencing of audit evidence: its impact on the extent of audit testing and report formulation, *Accounting and Business Research*, Vol. 22, No. 86, pp. 143-150.
Messier, W. F., Jr. and Plumlee, R. D. (1987), The effects of anticipation and frequency of errors on auditors' selection of substantive procedures, *Accounting and Business Research*, Vol. 17, No. 68, pp. 349-358.
Messier, W. F., Jr. and Tubbs, R. M. (1994), Recency effects in belief revision: the impact of audit experience and the review process, *Auditing: A Journal of Practice and Theory*, Vol. 13, No. 1, Spring, pp. 57-72.
Millichamp, A. H. (1990), *Auditing*, 5th edition, DP Publications Ltd, London.
Mock, T. J. and Wright, A. (1993), An exploratory study of auditors' evidential planning judgments, *Auditing: A Journal of Practice and Theory*, Vol. 12, No. 2, Fall, pp. 39-61.
Mock, T. J., Wright, A. M., Washington, M. T. and Krishnamoorthy, G. (1997), Auditors' uncertainty representation and evidence aggregation, *Behavioral Research in Accounting*, Vol. 9, Supplement, pp. 123-147.
Moeckel, C. (1990), The effect of experience on auditors' memory errors, *Journal of Accounting Research*, Vol. 28, No. 2, Autumn, pp. 368-387.
Moeckel, C. L. and Plumlee, R. D. (1989), Auditors' confidence in recognition of audit evidence, *The Accounting Review*, Vol. 64, No. 4, Oct., pp. 653-666.
Mynatt, C. R., Doherty, M. E. and Tweney, R. D. (1978), Consequences of confirmation and disconfirmation in a simulated research environment, *Quarterly Journal of Experimental Psychology*, Vol. 30, pp. 395-406.
Nisbett, R., Zukier, H. and Lumley, R. E. (1981), The dilution effect: nondiagnostic information weakens the implications of diagnostic information, *Cognitive Psychology*, Vol. 13, pp. 248-277.
Pei, B. K. W., Reckers, P. M. J. and Wyndelts, R. W. (1990), The influence of information presentation order on professional tax judgment, *Journal of Economic Psychology*, Vol. 11, pp. 119-146.

Pei, B. K. W., Reed, S. A. and Koch, B. S. (1992), Auditor belief revisions in a performance auditing setting: an application of the belief-adjustment model, *Accounting, Organizations and Society*, Vol. 17, No. 2, pp. 169-183.

Pennington, N. and Hastie, R. (1986), Evidence evaluation in complex decision making, *Journal of Personality and Social Psychology*, Vol. 51, No. 2, pp. 242-258.

Peters, J. M. (1990), A cognitive computational model of risk hypothesis generation, *Journal of Accounting Research*, Vol. 28, Supplement, pp. 83-103.

Popper, K. R. (1977), On hypotheses, In: *Thinking: Readings in Cognitive Science*, Johnson-Laird, P. N. and Wason, P. C. (eds.), Cambridge, England, Cambridge University Press, pp. 264-273.

Porter, B., Simon, J. and Hatherly, D. (1996), Principles of External Auditing, John Wiley and Sons, Chichester, England.

Power, M. (1992), From common sense to expertise: reflections on the prehistory of audit sampling, *Accounting, Organizations and Society*, Vol. 17, No. 1, pp. 37-62.

Power, M. (1995), Auditing, expertise and the sociology of technique, *Critical Perspectives on Accounting*, Vol. 6, pp. 317-339.

QSR. NUD.IST (1995), *User's Guide*, Qualitative Solutions and Research Pty Ltd.

Ricchiute, D. N. (1992), *Auditing*, 3rd edition, South-Western Publishing Co., Cincinnati, Ohio.

Salthouse, T. (1991), Expertise as the circumvention of human processing limitations, In : *Toward a General Theory of Expertise*, Ericsson, A. and Smith, J. (eds.), Cambridge, England, Cambridge University Press, pp. 286-300.

Sarantakos, S. (1993), *Social Research*, The Macmillan Press Ltd., Basingstoke, Great Britain.

Shaub, M. K. and Lawrence, J. E. (1996), Ethics, experience and professional skepticism: a situational analysis, *Behavioral Research in Accounting*, Vol. 8, Supplement, pp. 124-157.

Sherer, M. and Kent, D. (1983), *Auditing and Accountability*, Pitman Publishing Inc., Massachusetts.

Simon, D. and Francis, J. (1988), The effects of auditor change on audit fees: tests of price cutting and price recovery, *The Accounting Review*, Vol. 63, April, pp. 255-269.

Skov, R. B. and Sherman, S. J. (1986), Information-gathering processes: diagnosticity, hypothesis-confirmatory strategies, and perceived hypothesis confirmation, *Journal of Experimental Social Psychology*, Vol. 22, No. 2, March, pp. 93-121.

Smith, J. F and Kida, T. (1991), Heuristic and biases: expertise and task realism in auditing, *Psychological Bulletin*, Vol. 109, No. 3, May, pp. 472-489.

Spicer and Oppenheim, Mascarenras, A. and Turley, S. (1990), *Spicer's Practical Auditing*, Eighteenth edition, Butterworth, London.

Srull, T. K. (1981), Person memory: some test of associative storage and retrieval models, *Journal of Experimental Psychology: Human Learning and Memory*, Vol. 7, No. 6, November, pp. 440-463.

Staw, B. and Ross, J. (1987), Behavior in escalation situations: antecedents, prototypes, and solutions, In: *Research in Organizational Behavior*, Cummings, L. and Staw, B. (eds.), Greenwich, Connecticut, JAI Press, pp. 39-78.

Tan, H. (1995), Effects of expectations, prior involvement, and review awareness on memory for audit evidence and judgment, *Journal of Accounting Research*, Vol. 33, No. 1, Spring, pp. 113-135.

Trope, Y. and Bassok, M. (1982), Confirmatory and diagnosing strategies in social information gathering, *Journal of Personality and Social Psychology*, Vol. 43, No. 1, pp. 22-34.

Trope, Y. and Bassok, M. (1983), Information-gathering strategies in hypothesis-testing, *Journal of Experimental Social Psychology*, Vol. 19, pp. 560-576.

Trotman, K. T. and Wright, A. (1996), Recency effects: task complexity, decision mode, and task-specific experience, *Behavioral Research in Accounting*, Vol. 8, pp. 175-193.

Trotman, K. T. and Sng, J. (1989), The effect of hypothesis framing, prior expectations and cue diagnosticity on auditors' information choice, *Accounting, Organizations and Society*, Vol. 14, No. 5/6, pp. 565-576.

Troutman, C. M. and Shanteau, J. (1977), Inferences based on nondiagnostic information, *Organizational Behavior and Human Performance*, Vol. 19, pp. 43-55.

Tubbs, R. M., Gaeth, G. J., Lerine, I. P. and Osdol, L. A. V. (1993), Order effects in belief updating with consistent and inconsistent evidence, *Journal of Behavioral Decision Making*, Vol. 6, No. 4, pp. 257-269.

Tubbs, R. M., Messier, W. F., Jr. and Knechel, W. R. (1990), Recency effects in the auditor's belief-revision process, *The Accounting Review*, Vol. 65, No. 2, April, pp. 452-460.

Turley, S. and Cooper, M. (1991), *Auditing in the United Kingdom: A Study of Development in the Audit Methodologies in Large Accounting Firms*, Prentice Hall, New York.

Wallendael, L. R. V. and Guignard, Y. (1992), Diagnosticity, confidence, and the need for information, *Journal of Behavioral Decision Making*, Vol. 5, No. 1, pp. 25-37.

Waller, W. and Jiambalvo, J. (1984), The use of normative models in human information processing research in accounting, *Journal of Accounting Literature*, Vol. 3, pp. 201-223.

Wright, S. and Wright, A. M. (1997), The effect of industry experience on hypothesis generation and audit planning decisions, *Behavioral Research in Accounting*, Vol. 9, pp. 273-294.

Appendices

Appendix 1 - The Interview Schedule

General Information:

- Name
- Position
- Employer
- Qualifications
- Years of experience
- How long have you been working for the present firm?
- What was the previous employer? Big/ Medium/ Small
- How long have you worked for the previous employer?

Questions:

- What are the main steps of the audit process? How do you evaluate evidence? Are there any differences between new and continuing clients in this case?
- At what stage do you normally form an assumption or proposition or idea about the client's financial statements? Assumptions or propositions might be in the form of identifying a potential overstatement of assets or understatement of liabilities (Is this a sort of risk assessment?), or they might be the financial statement assertions themselves and in this case some subsidiary propositions could be driven from each assertion. What type of assumptions do you form? Do you document this assumption?
- What factors do you consider when forming an assumption or proposition? (Probes: size of client, how long company has been a client).
- When forming an assumption or proposition, do you usually formulate it entirely by yourself, or do other influences affect the way that you reach it? (Probes: depending on other sources like the firm's policy, client employees, another member of the audit team, decision aids, or superior's guidance).
- How committed will you feel to your assumption or proposition at the early stages? Does this ever vary? (Probes: Will this commitment differ according to the way you form your assumption or proposition?).
- Does your commitment to the initial assumption change over time or due to any other reasons?

- On your initial review of the financial statements, if you find any material changes what do you normally assume causes them ? (Probes: do you normally work on the assumption that there is an error in the financial statements or you will assume that there has been a change in the environment e.g. economical change, industrial change?).
- Do you think that expertise affects the way you formulate your initial assumption or proposition or your strategy in searching for evidence?
- Thinking about the evidence that affects your initial assumption or proposition, which type of evidence is most influential? (Probes: evidence supporting your initial assumption, evidence not supporting your initial assumption, or both types of evidence). Why? Will this depend on the way you formulate your initial assumption or proposition?
- Do you sometimes find pieces of evidence consistent with more than one proposition? (As an example of this type of evidence, evidence of zero errors in the sales transaction stream may be consistent with both a proposition that debtors are not overstated and that they are overstated). Do you prefer this type of evidence whether it supports your assumption or not? Why?
- What type of evidence will have the greatest effect on your initial assumption or proposition if you work on the assumption that there is an error in the financial statements (supporting/ not supporting/ both)? Will this differ if you work on the assumption that there has been a change in the environment?
- What other factors, in your opinion, can affect your search for evidence (time/ cost/ caution or conservatism/ other...)?
- Do you think that the order in which you receive pieces of evidence is important? In other words, which is most important to you; the first piece of evidence or the last piece?
- Do you normally look at all pieces of evidence together at the end of the search process or you prefer to look at pieces of evidence subsequently? Will these different strategies have different effects on your final opinion?

Appendix 2 - The Experimental Instrument: Group B-SbS

INTRODUCTION

This is a simulated auditing scenario of M Limited company. You are required to audit the debtors to check whether they are materially correct.
Please follow the steps outlined below in performing the work:

- You are provided with two booklets; one containing some background information and pieces of evidence from tests of controls and substantive tests. The other booklet contains your answer sheets.
- You will be asked to follow a certain approach in your evaluation of evidence. This approach involves forming an initial expectation about the debtors, in the form of a percentage, after reading the background information. You will then be asked to revise your chosen expectation once after evaluating all pieces of evidence from tests of controls, and then after evaluating all pieces of evidence from substantive tests.
- As you read through the background information and evidence provided you will be asked to do some work. Please do the work in the spaces provided on the answer sheets.

BACKGROUND

M Ltd specialises in the manufacturing of paper and cardboard. Its year-end is 31 March 1995. The auditors are starting their final audit on the 10th of April which should be completed by the end of the month. They have obtained copies of the 1995 accounts (actual and budget) together with actual results for previous years. The following information was available to you.

M Limited accounts: extracts from balance sheets

	Actual 31.3.93 £000	Actual 31.3.94 £000	Actual 31.3.95 £000	Budget 31.3.95 £000
Fixed assets	940	1,156	1,200	1,205
Current assets				
Stocks	407	441	373	427
Debtors	415	454	632	636
Due from subsidiaries	30	-	40	67
Bank and cash	101	-	-	8
	953	895	1045	1137
Current liabilities	694	751	833	875
Net current assets	259	144	212	262
Total net assets	1,199	1,300	1,412	1,467
Total capital and reserves	1,199	1,300	1,412	1,467

Extracts from profit and loss accounts

	Actual 31.3.93 £000	Actual 31.3.94 £000	Actual 31.3.95 £000	Budget 31.3.95 £000
Sales	3,769	3,949	3,936	4,153
Profit before tax	188	217	137	269
Taxation	85	86	48	93
Profit after tax	103	131	89	176
Dividends	20	30	10	40
Retained profit	83	101	79	136

Extract from overheads and expenses accounts

	Actual 31.3.93 £000	Actual 31.3.94 £000	Actual 31.3.95 £000	Budget 31.3.95 £000
Bad debt provision	4	2	6	3

The following information was also available to the auditors.

Extracts from permanent audit file; sales systems notes
1. The following schedule summarises key ratios for M Ltd since the year ended 31 March 1993.

		Actual		Budget
Key ratios	31.3.93	31.3.94	31.3.95	31.3.95
Debtors turnover	9.08	8.70	6.23	6.53
Average collection period	40.19	41.96	43.99	41.96

2. On despatch of the goods from the warehouse, a multi-part despatch note is raised:
Copy 1 goes to customer.
Copy 2 is retained in stores department to update records of stock levels.
Copy 3 is sent to sales invoicing department, used as basis for invoice and then filed with a copy invoice.
Despatch notes are sequentially numbered. Every period-end a check is performed to ensure that all despatch note numbers are accounted for, and any missing ones are followed up.

Sales Ledger
This is interfaced with the sales invoicing system so that as invoices are raised they are automatically posted to the ledger.
A print-out of the ledger is run every period-end giving details of every account.
Each customer is sent a monthly statement which is a duplicate of the sales ledger account.

Aged Debtors Listing
This is printed every month and shows the balance on each account broken down by the age of the unpaid invoices.

Credit Control
New customers are required to produce 2 references - from a bank and from a current supplier - before they are allowed credit. The amount allowed is decided by the credit controller.
The controller reviews the monthly aged listing and telephones customers whose balances include items more than 60 days old.
After items are more than 90 days old, a reminder letter is sent, with a sterner letter 14 days later. Three weeks thereafter, a late payer will receive a solicitor's letter and may eventually be sued.
The bad debt provision is 10% of debts over 90 days old.

Extracts from interim audit working papers

To test that all invoices represent despatches of goods and are arithmetically correct, a representative sample of 50 invoices for goods was selected. Details of goods via copy despatch notes to stock issue records were traced. Additions and calculations on each invoice were checked.

No errors were found. Hence, the conclusion was that all invoices relate to provision of goods and are arithmetically correct.

Now, you can turn to the answer sheets and enter your starting time on page 1. Then please answer the questions on that page.

Evidence from tests of controls

On evaluating the internal controls over the sales-debtors-collection cycle, the following evidence was obtained:

1st piece of evidence

In processing customer orders, credit approval is adequately segregated from the handling of cash receipts, as well as from the recordkeeping and sales functions.

2nd piece of evidence

The billing function is adequately segregated from the handling of cash receipts.

3rd piece of evidence

The handling of cash receipts is not adequately segregated from the debtors recordkeeping.

4th piece of evidence

Sales returns are not properly authorised.

Now, please do not turn the page until you revise (or form) your expectation in the space provided on the answer sheets page 2.

Evidence from substantive tests
1st piece of evidence
To test that debtors exist and are correctly stated, a representative sample of 25 sales ledger balances was selected. A letter was written to each customer requesting confirmation of his/her balance.
23 customers agreed on their balances.

2nd piece of evidence
From the previous 25 confirmations requested, 2 customers responded saying that they were unable to confirm their balances. The 2 balances add up to £20,000. Cash received after date to this point in time shows that 80% of these balances has been cleared, and the client assures you that these 2 customers are slow companies and the outstanding amounts are expected.

3rd piece of evidence
A review of the debtors showed that £70,000 are more than 60 days old of which £60,000 are more than 90 days old. However, none of the balances is individually material. The client made a general provision of £6000 for bad debts.

4th piece of evidence
To test that credit limits are not exceeded, a sample of 25 accounts was selected. The credit limit was compared with balance currently outstanding.
On review of the sales ledger it appeared that about 40% of account balances exceeded the stated credit limit.

5th piece of evidence
To test that credit is given only to approved customers, a sample of 25 new accounts opened this year was selected to check that 2 references had been taken up.
It was found that no references had been taken up for 5 customers.

6th piece of evidence
To test that all invoices are correctly posted to the correct customer's sales ledger account in the correct period, a representative sample of 30 sales invoices was selected. one invoice was found incorrectly posted. The error occured in a week where holiday cover was being provided. A further 10 invoices for that week were checked and no errors were found.

7th piece of evidence
To test that payments received from debtors are posted correctly to the sales ledger, a representative sample of 30 cheques received from debtors was selected from the cash book. The work done was to test that each had been posted to the correct debtor's account and matched to the invoices to which it related.
It was found that receipts are correctly posted to the sales ledger in accordance with the company's policy.

Now, please revise (or form) your expectation in the space provided on the answer sheets page 2.

Appendices

You can use page 3 of the answer sheets to write down any further analysis you would like to carry out. Then please give your final opinion by answering the questions on page 4.

Please write down your ending time on bottom of page 4 of the answer sheets.

For the purpose of statistical analysis please provide the information requested on page 5 of the answer sheets.

Thank you for your help

ANSWER SHEETS

> **Starting time:** ....

1. At this stage, can you form an initial expectation about whether debtors are materially correct?

    Yes   /   No

2. If no, please state reasons (then go to question 4).

3. If yes, please choose one of the following to be your expectation.
- Debtors are likely to be materially corrrect by -------%

(Please choose any number from 0 to 100 where 0% is very unlikely and 100% is very likely).
- What is your reason for choosing this expectation?

4. Do you consider the previous expectation (whether you have formed it or not) your risk assessment?

    Yes   /   No

5. If no, what is your risk assessment?

Evaluation of pieces of evidence

Please write down your evaluation of all pieces of evidence from tests of controls together and all pieces of evidence from substatntive tests together. *Please note that your evaluation is made by revising (or forming) your expectation.*

Evaluation of evidence from tests of controls

After having read all pieces of evidence from tests of controls, please revise (or form) your expectation.

Debtors are likely to be materially correct by ------- %

(Please choose any number from 0 to 100 where 0% is very unlikely and 100% is very likely).

Evaluation of evidence from substantive tests

After having read all pieces of evidence from substantive tests, please revise (or form) your expectation.

Debtors are likely to be materially correct by ------- %

(Please choose any number from 0 to 100 where 0% is very unlikely and 100% is very likely).

- You can use this page to write down any further analysis you would like to carry out.

The final opinion

- **At this stage, can you give your final opinion about the debtors?**

    Yes   /   No

If **yes**, what is your final opinion:

Please express this opinion in a percentage ranging from 0% to 100% (where 0% is very unlikely that debtors are materially correct and 100% is very likely).
.... %

- **What additional work, if any, do you think you have to carry out?**

- **What approximately would be the budgeted time for this additional work?**

Ending time: ....

Personal information

Any information you provide is confidential and will only be used for research purposes. However, for the purpose of statistical analysis please provide the following information about yourself.

Position in firm

                                                    Years   **Months**

Years of auditing experience

What was your degree subject?

Index

accounting research
  need for 138-40
  purpose 1
  studies 2
analytical procedures, American SAS No. 56 7, 9, 66
audit evidence
  centrality of 5
  classification, belief revision process 6-7
  evaluation, UK Auditing Standards 7-9
  research 5
  SAS UK 400 8, 78-9, 136
  strategies 6-7
  substantive procedures 8-9
  tests of control 8, 9
audit plan
  components 19
  model 20, 21
  SAS UK 200 9
audit process
  decision aids 35, 35-6
  description 19, 63
  effectiveness 103
  efficiency 103
  evidence 2, 3
  and initial belief 83-4
  stages 3, 4
  uncertainty 6
  US 69
audit risk model 77
  and belief-adjustment model 133
audit team
  and belief sources 79-80, 124
  research, need for 139
auditing
  decisions, and expertise 41-2, 124
  meaning 1
  research, need for 138-40
Auditing Practices Board, UK 136
auditors
  belief formation 33-4, 43
  confirmation bias 38-9, 85-9, 97
  dilution effect 40

  evidence evaluation 122-3, 125
  expectations 20
  knowledge structures 46
  memory 46, 138
  performance
    and environmental frame 37
    and error frame 37
  pressure on 5
  scepticism 44-5, 89-90, 97, 124
  and superiors' beliefs 35, 65

Bayes' theorem, and belief revision 7
belief
  alternative, forcing 37
  and diagnostic evidence 40
  formation
    auditor's 33-4, 43
    cognitive factors 46
    and expertise 42
    and professional scepticism 44-5
  generated 34
  inherited 34
    client's personnel 36
  initial
    and audit process 83-4
    and belief revision 78
    commitment to 65, 124
    concept 74-9, 123
    and decision aids 80-1
    examples 75-6
    formation 37, 64, 66, 73-84, 133-4
    and risk assessment 75-8, 85-6, 97, 115-17, 123, 131-4
  sources 34-6
    and audit team 79-80, 124
    research 35, 79-81
  superior's, and auditor's 35, 65
belief frame 36-8, 81-4
  and professional scepticism 44
  and search for evidence 37
  see also environmental frame; error frame

belief revision 5-6
    applicability 140
    and Bayes' theorem 7
    and belief-adjustment model 133
    and contrast/surprise model 7
    evidence classification 6-7
    and evidence evaluation 67, 121-40
    and expertise 42
    factors 47
    and initial belief 78
    interview data 121-2
    meaning 6, 33
    open-mind approaches
        EoS mode 128-9
        research 99-119, 127-9, 135
        SbS mode 128-9
    research 10, 49-61, 121-40
belief-adjustment model
    advantages 19-20, 22
    and audit risk model 133
    and belief revision 10, 133
    contrast/surprise model, comparison 17-18
    estimation tasks 25
    evaluation tasks 25
    formula 16-17
    order effect predictions 18-19
    predictions 15-16, 20
        validity 25-31
    research 19, 22
    studies 26-7
    see also contrast/surprise model

clients
    large/small, and evidence evaluation 71-2
    new/continuing, and evidence evaluation 69-71
cognitive consistency, meaning 45
cognitive factors
    belief formation 46
    and experience 46
confirmation bias, auditor's 38-9, 85-9, 97
contrast/surprise model
    and belief revision 7
    discounting model formula 14-15
    factors 13-14
    predictions
        studies 24
        validity 23-5
    see also belief-adjustment model

debtors scenario task 28
decision aids
    audit process 35-6
    and initial belief 80-1
decisions
    and memory 46
    and motivational factors 45-6
dilution effect 40
discounting model formula, contrast/surprise model 14-15

effectiveness, audit process 29, 103, 130, 137
efficiency
    audit process 29, 103, 130, 137
    and experience 84-5, 97
environmental frame 36, 81-2, 124
    and auditor's performance 37
EoS (end-of-sequence) mode
    evidence evaluation 94, 98, 126, 131
    open-mind approaches, belief revision 128-9
    see also SbS mode
error frame 36, 81, 82-3, 124
    and auditor's performance 37
estimation tasks, belief-adjustment model 25
evaluation tasks, belief-adjustment model 25
evidence
    diagnostic 39, 90, 97
        and belief 40
        meaning 40, 41
        and non-diagnostic evidence 40-1, 91, 124
    integration, difficulties 138
    order of 91-3, 97-8, 124-5, 126, 139
    SAS UK 400 8, 78-9, 136
    search for
        and belief frame 37
        and motivational factors 45-6
        and time/cost 95-6
    see also audit evidence; evidence evaluation
evidence evaluation

Index

auditors' approaches 122-3, 125
and belief revision 67, 121-40
EoS mode 94, 98, 126, 131
factors affecting 73-98, 123-6
findings 122-3
interview data 63-72, 121-2
large/small, clients 71-2
new/continuing clients 69-71
and open-mind approach 63-4, 68, 123, 127
SbS mode 93-4, 98, 126, 131
UK/US research 135-6
expectations, auditors 20
experience
and cognitive factors 46
and efficiency 84-5, 97
and recency effects 30, 44
see also expertise
expertise
and auditing decisions 41-2, 124
and belief formation 42
and belief revision 42
concept 41
drawbacks 42-3
and performance 41
see also experience

information seeking, strategies 40
interviews
evidence evaluation 63-72, 121-2
questions 151-2

knowledge structures, auditor's 46

Mann-Whitney U test 104, 105, 110
memory
auditor's 46, 138
and decision-making 46
models
audit planning 20, 21
belief-adjustment 10, 15-20, 22, 25-31, 133
contrast/surprise 7, 13-15, 23-5
motivational factors
and auditor's decisions 45-6
and search for evidence 45-6

open-mind

belief revision approaches
EoS mode 128-9
research 99-119, 135, 140
SbS mode 128-9
and evidence evaluation 63-4, 68, 123, 127
order effect predictions, belief-adjustment model 18-19

performance, and expertise 41
phenomenological approach, research 50
pilot testing 52-3, 59-60
positivistic approach, research 50
predictions, belief-adjustment model 15-16, 20

recency effects 25, 28, 29, 92
and experience 30, 44
research
auditing, need for 138-40
belief revision 10, 49-61, 121-40
analysis method 54
experimental design 55-6
experimental groups 58
experimental instrument 58-9, 153-64
experimental task 56-7
independent variables 57-8
interviews 52
open mind approaches 99-119
analysis method 101-2
benchmark opinion difference 107-8, 130
differences 102-9
discussion 108-9
evidence evaluation modes differences 109-15
expected additional time difference 105-6, 130
experiment time differences 103-5
experimental groups 100
final opinion difference 106-7
participants 100-1
participants 53-4, 56
phenomenological approach 50
pilot testing 52-3, 59-60
positivistic approach 50
research questions 50

    survey research 50-4
    belief-adjustment model 19, 22
    professional scepticism 44
review process 34
risk, SAS UK 300 77, 132
risk assessment
    example 76
    and initial belief 75-8, 85-6, 97, 115-17, 123, 131-4
    uncertainty 137
    see also audit risk model

sales-debtors cycle 23, 25
SAS (Statement of Auditing Standards)
    UK
        No. 200, audit planning 9
        No. 300, risk 77, 132
        No. 400, evidence 8, 78-9, 136
    US, No. 56, analytical procedures 7, 9, 66
SbS (step-by-step) mode
    belief revision, open-mind approaches 128-9
    evidence evaluation 93-4, 98, 126, 131
    see also EoS mode

scepticism
    auditor's 89-90, 97, 124
    and belief formation 44-5
    and belief frame 44
    meaning 44
    research 44
substantive procedures, audit evidence 8-9
survey research 50-4, 134-5

tests of control, audit evidence 8, 9
time/cost, and search for evidence 95-6

UK
    audit process, US, differences 72
    Auditing Practices Board 136
    Auditing Standards, evidence evaluation 7-9
    research, evidence evaluation 135-6
uncertainty, audit process 6
US
    audit process 69
    UK, differences 72
    research, evidence evaluation 135-6
    SAS No. 56, analytical procedures 136-7